D0117556

Get Test Smart!

THE ULTIMATE GUIDE TO **Middle School** STANDARDIZED TESTS

Laurie Rozakis, Ph.D.

SCHOLASTIC REFERENCE

An Imprint of

SCHOLASTIC

www.scholastic.com

ACKNOWLEDGMENTS

Writing books is very hard work, so it's a good thing that many people helped me work on this project! I could not have done it without them.

My deep gratitude to my dear editor Mary V. Jones for accepting my idea and working with me to develop the format. Mary, you are not only one of the smartest people I know, but also one of the nicest.

A tip of the hat to the wonderful people in Scholastic's design department, especially Becky Terhune. Thanks, too, to Carol Bobolts of Red Herring, who created the beautiful page layouts and art. They are true artists. Great thanks to the proofreaders led by Susan Jeffers Casel, who caught all those errors that I should have caught. To all these dedicated professionals, I am indebted to your wisdom, expertise, and devotion.

Library of Congress Cataloging-in-Publication Data available

ISBN-10: 0-439-87880-2
ISBN-13: 978-0-439-87880-7

10 9 8 7 6 5 4 3 2 1   07 08 09 10 11

Printed in the U.S.A.
First printing, February 2007
Book design by Red Herring Design

Contents

Chapter 1
9 Get Set for School Success

Chapter 2
23 Go for the Gold

Chapter 3
37 Work to Your Strengths

Chapter 4
45 Build Your Vocabulary for Standardized Tests

Chapter 5
57 Review Your Math Skills

Chapter 6
71 Improve Your English Skills

Chapter 7
83 Write Great Essays for Standardized Tests

A B C D E answer grid (filled bubble marked as ●)

1	A B C ● E	A B C ● E	A B C ● E	A B C ● E
2	● B C D E	● B C D E	● B C D E	● B C D E
3	● B C D E	● B C D E	● B C D E	● B C D E
4	A ● C D E	A ● C D E	A ● C D E	A ● C D E
5	A B C D ●	A B C D ●	A B C D ●	A B C D ●
6	A B C ● E	A B C ● E	A B C ● E	A B C ● E
7	A B ● D E	A B ● D E	A B ● D E	A B ● D E
8	A B ● D E	A B ● D E	A B ● D E	A B ● D E
9	A ● C D E	A ● C D E	A ● C D E	A ● C D E
10	A B C D ●	A B C D ●	A B C D ●	A B C D ●
11	A B C D ●	A B C D ●	A B C D ●	A B C D ●
12	A B C ● E	A B C ● E	A B C ● E	A B C ● E
13	● B C D E	● B C D E	● B C D E	● B C D E
14	● B C D E	● B C D E	● B C D E	● B C D E
15	A B ● D E	A B ● D E	A B ● D E	A B ● D E
16	A B C D ●	A B C D ●	A B C D ●	A B C D ●
17	A ● C D E	A ● C D E	A ● C D E	A ● C D E
18	A B C ● E	A B C ● E	A B C ● E	A B C ● E
19	● B C D E	● B C D E	● B C D E	● B C D E
20	A B ● D E	A B ● D E	A B ● D E	A B ● D E
21	A B C D ●	A B C D ●	A B C D ●	A B C D ●
22	A ● C D E	A ● C D E	A ● C D E	A ● C D E
23	A ● C D E	A ● C D E	A ● C D E	A ● C D E
24	A B ● D E	A B ● D E	A B ● D E	A B ● D E

CHAPTER 1

Sometimes it sounds like school has become a bowl of alphabet soup: PSAT, NAEP, MGA, CELLA, AP, and so much more! Each of these initials stands for a major standardized test. That's not to mention tests that have real names, like the Iowa tests and Stanford tests. Now that you're in middle school, you are most likely being bombarded with standardized tests. In fact, 46 states have already moved to higher standards. Each of these states administers a standardized test to help them assess their students' progress.

Get Set for Test Success

Middle school is a time of big changes. For instance, in elementary school, you stayed in the same classroom all day. You probably had the same teacher for every subject. But in middle school, you most likely have a complicated-looking schedule. It shows the different teachers you have for each class. You've got a locker, too. And a homeroom. Your middle school is probably a lot bigger than your elementary school. You'll meet many new kids. You'll have to study a lot more. What's the biggest change of all? There are so many more standardized tests... and they count a lot more. That's why these tests are often called "high-stakes assessments."

Why are there so many standardized tests in middle school?

For starters, education is more important now than it's ever been in the history of the world. As competition gets stiffer on the international stage, American schools are stepping up to the plate to prepare their graduates even better. Middle school is an ideal time to lay a strong foundation in testing skills. That's because standardized tests help middle schools prepare you for high school and college.

Second, they give parents a chance to know where their child stands. This helps parents keep up with their child's progress in school. Most important of all, standardized tests help ensure that you learn what you need to make your dreams and goals come true.

make your dreams and goals come true

Adjust Your Attitude

Parents, teachers, and our elected officials recognize the value of a standard measure of achievement. Right now, for example, the NAEP test is being given on a sample basis. "NAEP" stands for the National Assessment of Educational Progress. It's given in 43 states for state scores. The goal is to make a test personalized so parents will know how their child stands. Some people want to make the NAEP mandatory throughout the country.

Then we have the TIMS test. "TIMS" stands for Teaching Integrated Math and Science. It's an international test on math and science. It's being given all over the country, too. The TIMS test helps schools measure your progress against that of kids in other countries. This helps schools adjust their curriculum to meet—and exceed—what's being taught to kids your age all over the world.

These standardized tests, and others like them, can help you do your best. But you have to take control of your learning and make a commitment to succeed. In middle school, you're expected to work more on your own. It's now your job to track your own progress. You have to study more and get extra help when you need it. *But don't wait until the day of the test to find out that you don't understand the material.* By then, you'll have to scramble to catch up.

Decide that you can succeed. Decide that you'll work hard to do well on standardized tests and achieve your goals. Having a positive attitude makes school easier and more fun. Being proactive and positive can make a huge difference on your scores on standardized tests.

Self Test

People have a lot of strange ideas about standardized tests. How good are you at telling test truth from test fiction? Take this test to see what you know about studying and tests. Write True if the sentence is true. Write False if the sentence is false.

.... 1. **You can study for a classroom test but not for a standardized test.**

.... 2. **People are born knowing how to study.**

.... 3. **By middle school, kids know how to study.**

.... 4. **If you're smart, you don't have to study.**

.... 5. **Once you learn something, you don't have to practice it.**

ANSWERS

1. *False!* Some people think that you can't study for a standardized test because you have no way of knowing what will be on the test. These people are wrong. You can—and should—study for all tests, especially standardized tests. You can study for standardized tests by doing all your class work, getting to know the test format, and taking practice tests. You can review your math skills, too. You can also do a lot of reading to increase your speed and understanding.

2. *False!* No one is born knowing how to study. Studying is a skill, just like driving a car or hanging wallpaper. Since it is a skill, studying can be learned. It's not that difficult, either.

3. *False!* Many middle school kids don't know how to study. Some kids never studied in elementary school. Other kids don't know how to approach the material. They waste time and get frustrated. So don't be worried if you're not sure you know how to study. You have a lot of company!

4. *False!* Intelligence has nothing to do with studying. Everyone has to study. Some scholars are trying to answer the question: "When a person is very good at something, what makes the person good at it?" Anders Ericsson, a psychology professor at Florida State University, has been studying this question for more than thirty years. Ericsson started by training people to memorize a series of numbers. At first, the average person could remember 7 to 20 numbers. After 200 hours of practice, the same person could remember over 80 numbers. From these experiments and others, Ericsson concluded that memorizing is a matter of repetition. The best way to learn facts, Ericsson concluded, is by going over the material again and again. This means that you get very good at something by study and practice.

5. *False!* Once you learn something, you do have to practice it. Ericsson and the people he works with concluded that experts are made, not born. Outstanding athletes, dancers, musicians, doctors, and students became experts by practicing. Their conclusion: "Practice *does* make perfect!" *To do well in school, you need the desire to do well. You need to work hard. Most of all, you need to study, learn, and practice these skills.*

Practice does make perfect!

Middle school *is* a time of big changes. This means that it's a good time to make any changes that can help you do your best. Now, let's explore some things that have a big effect on standardized test success. ...things you might never have considered.

Get Enough Sleep

As you read at the beginning of this chapter, middle school is a lot different from elementary school. First, you probably have to get up a lot earlier now! Yawn. This means that you have to get to bed earlier at night and get a full night's sleep. *Are you sleeping enough? Take this quiz to see. Rank your answers from 1 to 4. After you take the quiz, total up your score.*

1 = would never doze off
2 = slight chance of dozing
3 = average chance of falling asleep
4 = strong chance of falling asleep

SCORE YOURSELF
10-15 points You're probably getting enough sleep at night.
16+ points You're probably *not* getting enough sleep at night

SITUATION	CHANCE OF FALLING ASLEEP
In class	
During a test	
In study hall	
In the school cafeteria	
While reading	
While studying at home	
At the movies	
At a school play	
On the school bus	
At night, when it's bedtime	
TOTAL	

HOW MUCH SLEEP DO YOU NEED?

Although everyone needs different amounts of sleep to function at their best, kids in middle school need at least nine hours of sleep every night to function well. That's more sleep than adults need! (Adults need about eight hours of sleep a night.)

Most middle schools start around 7:30AM. *What time do you have to be asleep to get at least nine hours of sleep?* Do the math: To wake up in time to wash, eat breakfast, and get to school by 7:30, you need to be asleep by 9:30PM. Follow these hints for winding down at the end of the evening:

WAYS TO SLEEP BETTER

1. *Don't surf the Internet or watch action movies before bed.* They help you stay awake instead of letting you relax.

2. *Instead, do settling-down activities, such as reading a book.*

3. *After dinner, don't drink beverages that have caffeine because they can keep you awake.* Avoid colas, coffee, and tea.

4. *Exercise regularly, too, since it helps relax your muscles.* But exercise before bed actually keeps you awake, so allow at least two hours after exercise before you go to sleep for the night. That means you should plan on finishing your soccer game by 7:00 if you plan to be asleep by 9:00PM.

5. *Try going to bed at the same time each night and waking up at the same time each morning.* Getting into a sleep routine helps signal your body to relax. Don't sleep late on the weekends, since over-sleeping can keep you awake the next night.

Do the math!

you are what

Exercise Regularly

Research shows that kids who play sports or who are physically active do better in school. However, only about 38 percent of all middle-schoolers get enough exercise.

Design an exercise program that builds your strength, flexibility, and endurance. Consider the exercises that enable you to build skill-related and health-related fitness. Here are some tips to help you design your program:

2 **If you haven't exercised much, see your health care provider for a physical exam first.**

Choose exercises that you enjoy so you'll have fun. If exercising is fun, you'll be more likely to stick with the program for life.

"You are what you eat," the old saying goes—and it's true. Food gives you the fuel you need to pay attention in class, to study, and to do your best on tests. ***But how do you know what foods to eat? And how do you know how much of each food to eat?*** The government to the rescue!

In 1992, the United States Department of Agriculture developed a great tool to help everyone make good food choices. It's called the Food Guide Pyramid. You can find it on the web at **http://www.mypyramid.gov.** Each person has a Pyramid that is right for them based on their age, gender, and level of physical activity level. The Food Pyramid helps you learn how to eat the foods you need for a balanced diet. It guides you toward healthy foods, including dark green vegetables like spinach, kale, and broccoli. You'll learn about orange vegetables and legumes, too. Fruits, whole grains, and low-fat milk products are also important parts of nutritious eating.

The following worksheet from MyPyramid can help you become more aware of your food choices. Complete the worksheet to help you set healthy food goals.

Eating well is key as you prepare for a standardized test. Since these tests are long and important, you need to be well-nourished and in top shape. You can't do your best if you don't have the right fuel in your belly, bones, and body!

If you feel any significant pain while exercising, stop immediately. Consult your health care provider before resuming your exercise program.

My Pyramid Worksheet

Check how you did yesterday and set a goal to aim for tomorrow

Write In Your Choices From Yesterday	Food and Activity	Tip
Breakfast:	**Grains**	Make at least half your grains whole grains.
Lunch:	**Vegetables**	Color your plate with all kinds of great tasting veggies.
Snack:	**Fruits**	Make most choices fruit, not juice.
Dinner:	**Milk**	Choose fat free or low fat most often.
Snack:	**Meat and Beans**	Choose lean meat and chicken or turkey. Vary your choices—more fish, beans, peas, nuts, and seeds.
Physical activity:	**Physical activity**	Build more physical activity into your daily routine at home and school.

How did you do yesterday? ☐ Great ☐ So-So ☐ Not So Great

My food goal for tomorrow is: _____

My activity goal for tomorrow is: _____

Name: _____

My Pyramid
FOR KIDS

Goal (Based On a 1800 Calorie Pattern)	List Each Food Choice In Its Food Group*	Estimate Your Total
6 ounce equivalents (1 ounce equivalent is about 1 slice bread, 1 cup dry cereal, or ½ cup cooked rice, pasta, or cereal)		_____ ounce equivalents
2½ cups (Choose from dark green, orange, starchy, dry beans and peas, or other veggies)		_____ cups
1½ cups		_____ cups
3 cups (1 cup yogurt, or 1 ½ ounces cheese = 1 cup milk)		_____ cups
5 ounce equivalents (1 ounce equivalent is 1 ounce meat, chicken, turkey, or fish, 1 egg, 1 T. peanut butter, ½ ounce nuts, on ¼ cup dry beans)		_____ ounce equivalents
At least **60 minutes** of moderate to vigorous activity a day on most days.		_____ minutes

*Some foods don't fit into any group. These "extras" may be mainly fat or sugar—limit your intake of these.

Self Test

What are your school strengths?
What things do you want to improve?
Take this simple test to see. Be honest.
Think about ways you can maximize your chances for
earning a high score on all your standardized tests.

THINGS I DO WELL IN SCHOOL

1. *List two things you're really good at.*

....

....

2. *List two reasons why you like school.*

....

....

3. *List your two favorite subjects.*

....

....

4. *List two things you can say to make you feel good about school.*
   FOR EXAMPLE: "I'm smart in math."

....

....

....

**THINGS I NEED TO IMPROVE IN SCHOOL
TO PUMP UP MY STANDARDIZED TEST SCORES**

1. *Do all my school work and homework.*

2. *Concentrate more and pay attention in class.*

3. *Take good notes.*

4. *Take standardized tests seriously.*

5. *Stay calm during standardized tests.*

6. *Read more.*

7. *Improve my memory.*

8. *Work to my strengths.*

9. *Understand my learning style.*

10. *Learn more vocabulary.*

11. *Get better at math.*

12. *Review capitalization.*

13. *Brush up on punctuation.*

14. *Improve my spelling.*

15. *Master grammar and usage.*

16. *Learn how to take objective standardized tests.*

17. *Unlock the secrets to document-based tests.*

18. *Discover how to write great essays under pressure.*

19. *Practice all the standardized test skills
covered in this book.*

20. *Be all I can be!*

WHERE CAN I FIND HELP IN THIS BOOK?

This book can't help you unlock your locker, but it *can* help you unlock your potential. It can't help you find your homeroom, but it *can* help you study smarter, not harder. Here's how to use it:

Chapter 2 covers information about doing all your school work and homework. In this chapter, you'll also learn how to take good notes. *Chapter 3 teaches you to take standardized tests seriously, stay calm during standardized tests, and prepare by reading more.* This chapter also helps you learn how to improve your memory and work to your strengths by finding your specific learning style or styles. *In Chapter 4, you'll improve your vocabulary.* This is a crucial skill for just about every standardized test because they all involve reading—even the math tests! And while we're on math…

Chapter 5 reviews math skills. Soon, you'll take standardized tests that are completely on math, such as the Advanced Placement math tests. You'll also learn about standardized tests that have large math portions, such as the Preliminary SAT®/National Merit Scholarship Qualifying Test. This is a standardized test designed to give you practice for the SAT Reasoning Test™, the college admissions test. The PSAT/NMSQT measures critical reading skills, math problem-solving skills, and writing skills. Not all colleges require the SAT, but most do. Your score is one factor colleges use to weigh your chances of success there. This helps them decide whether or not to admit you.

The PSAT also gives you a chance to enter the National Merit Scholarship Corporation (NMSC) scholarship program. Some students don't take this test until the ninth or tenth grade, but other students take it as early as the sixth grade. According to Margot Adler, writing in *All Things Considered*, "These days, more than 100,000 students are taking the SAT while they're still in middle school. Some are under increasing pressure to get ready for college, no matter how early. And some want to qualify for prestigious academic summer programs such as the one at Johns Hopkins University." (May 4, 2006).

Chapter 6 helps you improve your English skills by reviewing capitalization, punctuation, spelling, grammar, and usage. Along with Chapter 7, this will help you learn how to write great essays. Many standardized tests given on state and national levels now have writing sections. *Chapter 8 teaches you how to take objective tests, including multiple-choice questions.* Most standardized tests follow this format. *Chapter 9 covers doing your best on document-based questions (DBQs).* These tests require you to read and scrutinize historical documents. Then you write an essay on them. *Chapter 10 gives you a lot more practice taking standardized tests.*

You know a lot more than you think you know!
Now, let's pull it all together to make it easier for you to do your best on standardized tests.

CHAPTER
2

Go for the
Gold

The class bell rings.
Where are you?

Put a check next to your answer:

.... *Fighting with your locker, which still refuses to open.*

.... *Styling your hair in the bathroom.*

.... *Dashing down the hall toward the classroom.*

.... *Standing in the back of the room, copying someone's homework.*

.... *Sitting in your seat, ready to get to work.*

Go with that last choice. Being ready to learn reduces stress. It sends a powerful message to your teacher that you take your studies seriously. Best of all, it helps you succeed. This chapter will show you some ways to do better in school—and enjoy school more. These skills set the stage for victory on standardized tests.

Be a Serious Student.

Learning is like saving money: the more you put into the bank, the more you get out. Here are some good ways to get more from school. Each of these suggestions will help you be a better student. You'll do better on all your standardized tests, too.

1. *Have excellent attendance.*
You can't win it if you're not in it! Of course you'd never go to class if you're really ill. But sometimes, you wake up feeling a bit wonky but in an hour or two you're doing better. Give it the benefit of the doubt and come to class.

2. *Get to class early.*
You know the famous saying: "The early bird catches the worm." The saying is famous because it's true: the person who arrives early usually does better than the person who dashes in at the last moment. Leave yourself enough time to get to class and to tests. Being late to class makes it harder to learn. Being late to a standardized test can make you miss crucial directions and lose valuable time. You may not even be allowed to take the test if you are late.

be the *early* *bird*

3. *Sit in the front row.*
If you get to choose your own seat, pick one in the front of the room. Sitting in the front helps you focus on the real action—the teacher and the blackboard. Sitting in the back helps you zone off…which you don't want to do. Where you choose to sit sounds like a small thing, but it can make a surprisingly big difference in how well you learn.

4. *Participate in class.*
Raise your hand when you have the answer. It shows the teacher that you're interested. It shows that you are making an effort to understand the material. It helps you and the teacher figure out what you understand…and what you don't. Most important of all, paying attention shifts your brain into gear. When you participate, you learn more. You remember it better, too.

5. *Be an active learner.*
Pay close attention. Make eye contact with the teacher. Show that you are listening. Even if you don't raise your hand all the time, signal your understanding by focusing on the teacher and the board. Take notes, too.

6. *Turn off your cell phone.*
Don't even leave it on vibrate. Whether or not you carry your cell, pretend that you don't. That way, you won't be distracted by calls. You're in school to learn. Excessive socializing takes too much time away from school.

Take Standardized Tests Seriously

Of course, standardized tests don't determine the kind of person you are. But they do help you achieve your goals and make your dreams come true. Go into every standardized test completely prepared. Follow these hints to do your best on standardized tests:

1. *Keep up with the test news.*
Know when all the standardized tests are given. Understand what each one means for you now, and in the future. Sometimes the school will automatically register you for a standardized test, but other times you will have to register through a teacher or the guidance department. If you want to take a standardized test that's not given at your middle school—such as the PSAT for admissions to a special academic summer program—make sure to submit your application in time. (Some standardized tests allow late registration, but they charge a stiff fee. Ouch!)

2. *Come to every test prepared.*
Have the right equipment: calculator, batteries, watch, pens, pencils, and whatever else you need. Most standardized tests require you to have identification, too, so be sure to bring your school ID.

3. *Choose your seat carefully.*
Stay away from people who will distract you. Sit close to people who want to do well, as you do.

relax

4. *Read the directions all the way through.*
Restate the directions in your own words to make sure you know what you have to do.

5. *Use your time effectively.*
Spend the most time on the questions that count the most. Spend the least time on the questions that count the least. Pace yourself so you keep on working steadily.

6. *Do your best.*
Who doesn't get frustrated during a standardized test and want to walk out of the room? But keep plugging away and finish the test. These tests usually get easier as you go along because you get into a routine and set up a rhythm.

7. *Show up!*
This sounds silly, but some people try to avoid as many standardized tests as they can. Standardized tests *can* bring on a nasty case of nerves. As a result, it's tempting to stay home, even if you're registered for the test and all set to go. "I'll catch the next test," you think. "After all, the test is given six times a year." Some important standardized tests *are* given several times a year, but others are a one-shot deal. Even if you're nervous, be sure to show up for every standardized test you have to take. Here's the bonus: the more high-stakes tests you take, the easier they get.

8. *Be positive.*
Don't beat yourself up if your score isn't what you expected. You'll do better next time. After all, you have this book to help you!

Test anxiety can make it hard for even the best prepared student to do well. Don't get upset if some questions seem harder than others. They probably are. Don't get upset if you can't get some answers. Just keep working. If you have time, you can return to these questions later. Here are some more hints:

USE A TEST STRATEGY

Decide how to tackle the test. For instance, you can work from the beginning to the end of the test. Answer every question. Put a question mark next to any questions you think are incorrect. If you have time, return to these questions later. Or, you can answer all the easy questions first. Then go back to the test and answer as many difficult questions as you can in the time you're allowed. You might write the essay first and then do the multiple-choice questions. *Choose the strategy that works best for the test and your comfort level.*

BREATHING EXERCISES

Stop working for a moment to relax. Take some deep breaths. Calm yourself down.

VISUALIZE A BEAUTIFUL SCENE

Along with breathing exercises, focusing on a calming scene can help you relax. Imagine a sandy beach with the waves lapping slowly on the shore. Or try thinking of a campground ringed by protective mountains. Imagine this serene landscape for a moment or two. Then back to work!

Do All Your Schoolwork

Maybe you don't like the teacher. "The teacher is too hard/too easy/too unprepared," you say. So you and the teacher have a personality clash. Or maybe you don't like the subject. "I'll never use French/math/biology/social studies/whatever," you claim. Perhaps you will and perhaps you won't.

Remember that teachers are human. Some teachers will like you. Others won't. That's life. But all teachers will give you the benefit of the doubt. If you make an effort to do your best, they'll do their best to help you.

You can't predict the future, but you *can* control the present. Take charge of your life. Be disciplined. Tell yourself, "I must do my work. My schoolwork matters a lot. I must prepare for standardized tests. It's up to me to make the choice to succeed." Take pride in what you can achieve when you set your mind to it.

Do All Your Homework

Of course you should do all your homework, but it's not always that easy. These hints can help you get your homework done.

1. **Break the assignments into small pieces.** They'll be easier to get done. For instance, study five words at a time, rather than fifty. Then the task won't be as daunting.

2. **Analyze the assignments so you understand them.** Before you start, read the entire task. Figure out how it fits with what you're learning in class. Be sure you understand what you're supposed to be learning.

3. **Do the important assignments first.** For example, study for the social studies test you have tomorrow rather than working on the art project due next week.

4. **Try to get your homework done when you first get home.** Putting it off just makes it harder to get it done.

5. **Write down all your assignments so you remember what you have to do.**

6. **Don't take on too many activities.** It's hard to get two or three hours of homework done when you have Student Council, home chores, and soccer practice. Homework comes first.

7. **Set up a quiet place to study.** Turn off the television, radio, and iPod.

8. **Pace yourself.** Study for about 30-45 minutes at a time. Then take a 10-minute break before starting again.

9. **Remember that teachers give homework for a reason.** They know you need the practice.

10. **Use all your time.** If you have study hall, spend it getting some homework done. Use even the little chunks of time. For example, proofread your English essay while you're riding the subway or bus to school.

Take Good Notes

There are different ways to take good notes. Choose the method that works best for you. You can make up your own method, too, by combining some of the methods below.

THE TWO-COLUMN METHOD
Divide your notebook paper into two columns. On the right, make a big column. On the left, make a small column, about one inch wide. Take notes in the big column. Highlight important concepts, facts, and main headings in the small column.

THE SPLIT PAGE METHOD
Divide your notebook paper in two equal columns. Take notes in the right column. After class, outline the material in the left column.

THREE COLUMN METHOD
Divide your notebook paper into three equal columns. Take notes in the first

Listen Up!

In the novel *The Joy Luck Club*, one of the characters says, "My mother used to say, 'Auntie Ying is not hard of hearing. She is hard of listening.'" The author of *The Joy Luck Club* knew that listening isn't the same as hearing. ***Study this chart to see the difference:***

HEARING	LISTENING
Sound waves hit the nerves in the ear. *Passive process*	***The brain takes meaning from the sound waves.*** *Active process*

DIFFERENT TYPES OF LISTENING

Listening is crucial to learning. That's because much of the information in middle school is given orally. For example, the teacher lectures in math class. An author gives a presentation in English. The coach explains the game directions in physical education. Listening and learning go together.

In class, your goal is to get as much information as you can. But listening isn't as easy as it sounds. You can go through an entire day sitting at your desk, looking at the teacher, nodding at the right moments—yet not be listening at all.

One of the keys to succeeding on standardized tests is good listening. That's because you must make sure that you understand the task and the directions. **Good listening can really help you do your best on high-stakes tests.**

column. After class, outline the material in the second column. Write any questions or additional information in the third column.

TAKE GROUP NOTES

Form a group with two other classmates. Take turns taking notes. On the days you are not taking notes, listen extra carefully in class. Participate in class and ask questions about information you don't understand. After class, get a copy of the group notes. Better yet, recopy them yourself. Add any information that's missing. Share your new notes with the group.

You may want to tape record lectures. Always get your teacher's permission first. But take notes as well.

Test Words

Standardized tests have a language all their own. When you understand the words used on the tests, you'll know what you have to do. Below are the key words you'll encounter most on standardized tests.

1. ***Recall:*** *to remember information.* When you recall, you show that you have learned facts, details, and formulas. On a standardized test, for example, you might be asked to define vocabulary words you learned or apply math formulas.

2. ***Analyze:*** *to separate an idea into parts and understand how the parts are related to each other.* When you analyze, you show that you have read the passage and understand what it means. On a standardized test, you might be asked to analyze a passage on a process such as condensation, or the causes and effects of a historical event, such as the Civil War.

3. ***Classify:*** *to sort into groups.* When you classify, you place similar objects together. You might be given a classification system or have to create one on your own. On a standardized test, you might be asked to classify words based on their roots or meanings.

4. ***Compare and contrast:*** *to show how two topics are similar (compare) or different (contrast).* On a standardized essay test, you might be asked to compare and contrast two novels, two pets, or two places, etc.

5. ***Evaluate:*** *to examine and judge carefully.* Evaluating asks you to apply your beliefs to the topic. You must support your opinion with facts, details, examples, and quotes from experts in the field. On a standardized essay test, you might be asked to evaluate if all students should be required to wear uniforms, if fast food should be sold in school, or if voting should be conducted over the Internet.

6. ***Summarize:*** *to rewrite something in your own words*. Summaries are always shorter than the original documents. Summaries show your ability to find the main ideas and key details. On a standardized test, you might be asked to identify the best summary of a passage on an ancient African kingdom or the structure and function of cells.

knowledge = power

Know All About the Test

You wouldn't set off on a trip without a map. You wouldn't walk into a standardized test without knowing what's likely to be on it either. Getting information about a standardized test is like getting a good map. You'll know what to study and how much time to spend on each subtopic. Then you won't be lost.

When you're preparing to take a standardized test, go over previously-given tests so you know the format. Your teacher may give you these tests to use for practice. If not, you can often get previously-given tests in review books or on-line.

Practice tests help you focus your studying. The process can look like this:

1

STEP #1
Take a practice test so you know what topics are most likely to be tested.

2

STEP #2 *Study your notes and textbooks on those topics.*

3

STEP #3
Take another practice test.

4

STEP #4
Study the topics you got wrong.

REPEAT STEPS 3 AND 4 UNTIL YOU GET THE SCORE YOU WANT. Try to aim for at least 15 points higher than the score you want. That gives you enough wiggle-room to earn the score you need.

USE THIS CHECKLIST TO PREPARE FOR A STANDARDIZED TEST:

What material will be on the standardized test?

How long is the standardized test?

How many questions does the standardized test have?

How much does each question count?

Will I lose credit for guessing?

What format are the questions? (multiple choice, essay, etc.)

Will the test be paper-and-pen or computer?

Will I be able to ask questions during the standardized test?

How will the standardized test be used? Does it determine if I have to attend summer school or get extra help, for instance?

Read!

One of the best ways to prepare for any standardized test is by reading. "How can reading a novel help me on a standardized test?" you may ask. Reading novels, short stories, and nonfiction for pleasure helps you learn vocabulary, understand the author's message, analyze information in a text, and read more fluently. These skills are especially important for state and national standardized tests.

You should read for pleasure at least half an hour to an hour a day.

Some standardized tests even assign a reading list based on your test score. For example, the California English-Language Arts Standards Test has different reading lists for students in grades K-12. There's a special reading list just for students in grades 6-8. The California test educators know that reading can help you not only do your best on standardized tests, but also become a life-long learner.

Use a Study Schedule.

	MONDAY
Class	
Homework	
Chores	
Phone	
Internet	
TV	
Sports	
Shopping	
Meals	
Grooming	
Sleep	
Other	

become a life-long learner

While we're on the topic of time…"I don't have enough time to study," you may say. Time does have a way of slipping away.

How do you use your time?
Write down how much time you spend doing the following activities:

TUESDAY	WEDNESDAY	THURSDAY	FRIDAY	WEEKEND

What activities can you cut to increase your study time?
Making a study schedule can help you figure it out. Study 15 minutes a day for an easy class, half an hour a day for an average class, and an hour a day for a difficult class. **Use the form on the following page. Write the amount of time you need to study each day. Make a new schedule for each week to help you keep up with assignments.**

	MONDAY	TUESDAY	WEDNESDAY	THURSDAY
English				
Math				
Science				
Social Studies				
Foreign Language				

Set challenging but reasonable goals. For example, it's reasonable to study two hours a day for an important standardized test. It's not reasonable to study five hours a day for the same test. You should start studying months ahead, too. For an important standardized test, allow yourself at least six months of concentrated study.

But don't beat yourself up if you can't keep up with your schedule. Rework your schedule and activities so both are more reasonable.

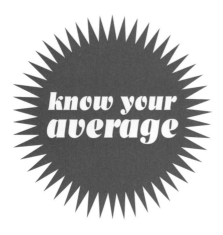

know your **average**

Check Your Grades.

It's easy to lose track of your grades in middle school. However, knowing your average will help you monitor your progress. Here's how to best track your grades:

✴ ***Keep copies of all your tests.***
If the teacher wants the test back, write down your grade so you have a record.

✴ ***Talk to your teacher.*** You may not know how much each test counts. Without this information, you may not be able to figure out your average. Make an appointment to meet when you are both free.

Get Help

If you don't understand something in class, get help right away. Follow these steps:

1. *Ask your teacher.*

That's a teacher's job! Most teachers are required to offer extra help. It may be before or after school. Let your teacher know you are coming for extra help. Make a list of concepts that you find confusing. This will help you use the time wisely. Bring your notes and books. Go over your notes, so your teacher can see if you copied something down incorrectly. Most of the time, even half an hour of one-on-one explanation can straighten out the problems.

2. *Review the books and your notes.*

After you go for extra help, reread the textbook and your notes. Summarize the information in your own words. Reviewing the material this way helps you remember it.

3. *Ask your parents.*

Some parents remember a lot of what they learned in middle school. They may even be experts in the field. Even if they are not, getting their ideas helps you look at the information in a new way.

4. *Ask your older brothers and sisters.*

If you are lucky enough to have older siblings, ask them to go over confusing problems with you. After all, they took the same classes a few years ago.

5. *Get a tutor.*

Often, honor society members tutor for free. In many schools, you can ask teachers other than your own for extra help as well. You may even want to hire a tutor to go over the material a few times until you master it.

No matter whom you ask for extra help, remember: you are asking for help. You're not asking them to do your work for you. That's not helping you at all!

This may seem like a lot to digest all at once, so read this chapter over a few times. Review these hints when you have a spare moment, too, especially before a standardized test.

CHAPTER 2: **Go for the Gold**

CHAPTER

3

Work

to Your
Strengths

Which of these students best describes you?

Chloe loves to work in groups. Ben is just the opposite: he is easily distracted and can't remember anything when he works with others. Logan can memorize anything if he puts the information into a song. Ebony could read before she started school; however, she has a difficult time in math. Jacinta is always taking things apart and putting them back to together. She learns best by figuring things out on her own.

One of the keys to success on standardized tests is figuring out how you learn.
Then you can use your time much more productively. You'll learn more in less time. That's what this chapter is all about.

Memorize Facts for Standardized Tests

As you discovered in Chapter 2, most standardized tests require you to use the information you've learned to classify, compare and contrast, analyze, or evaluate a topic. In addition, all standardized tests ask you to recall information that you should have memorized. For example, you need to know formulas and equations to solve the math items on standardized tests. Further, you must know word definitions to get the correct answers on vocabulary and reading comprehension items on standardized tests. This is true on the PSAT, for instance. It's also important to have memorized the dates of historical events to place those events in the right order on social studies tests. Here are two other examples:

* The MGA, the Middle Grades Assessment, is a standardized test designed for eighth grade students. This test, administered by the Educational Testing Service, has three parts: a student survey, a transcript study, and achievement tests in math, science, and reading. The achievement tests in math, science, and reading assess what you have learned, so you must know facts to do well.

* The NAEP, the National Assessment of Educational Progress, is a standardized test designed for fourth, eighth, and twelfth grade students. You read about this test in Chapter 1. The NAEP is also administered by the Educational Testing Service. As a middle school student, you'll take the NAEP in eighth grade. The NAEP has sections on many core subjects, including reading, math, science, and writing. This test is given in so many states that it's gotten the nickname "The Nation's Report Card."

study and know the subjects

Memorization is especially important for earning a high score on state standardized tests. The California Standards Tests (CSTs) and the Florida Comprehensive Assessment Test ® (FCATs), for instance, ask questions on specific subjects including math, vocabulary, social studies, science, and grammar. The U.S. Department of Education's Educational Resources Information Center on Assessment and Evaluation says: "The best way to prepare for tests—whether they're teacher-made or standardized—is to study and know the subjects."

Beef Up Your Memory!

This means you have to memorize information. Fortunately, memorization doesn't have to be difficult. Just use the methods below. Choose the ones that work best for you. You'll surely find some that are fun and easy.

TOP TEN WAYS TO MEMORIZE

1 Make Words.

Take the first letter of each word and make it into a word. Here are some well-known examples:

Use these examples and other well-known ones. You can make up your own, too.

WORD	WHAT IT STANDS FOR	WHAT IT HELPS YOU REMEMBER
ROY G BIV	red, orange, yellow, green, blue, indigo, violet	*the colors of the rainbow*
HOMES	Huron, Ontario, Michigan, Erie, Superior	*the five Great Lakes*
FACE	F, A, C, E	*The spaces on the G clef in music*

2 Make a Sentence.

If you can make a word to help you memorize ideas, why not a sentence? The following sentence helps you remember the notes on the lines on the G-clef: *Every Good Boy Deserves Fun.* Look at the first letter in each word. You'll realize that the notes are E, G, B, D, and F.

3 Rhyme It.

Making a rhyme helps you remember facts, too. For example, Henry VIII had six wives. The following rhyme helps you remember what happened to each wife, in order: Divorced, beheaded, died; Divorced, beheaded, survived.

Sing It.

How did you memorize the alphabet? You learned the ABC song! Use this memory idea with other new information, too. Set the information to music. The information will be even easier to remember if the song rhymes.

Teach It.

Once you get the idea, explain it to yourself or to someone else in your own words. You can even teach it to an imaginary audience. This forces you to organize the material in a way that makes sense to you. It also helps you anticipate questions that will be on the test. As a bonus, you'll be able to correct any misunderstandings you have.

Link It.

Link a word or image to the material you want to recall. The image helps you remember the idea. For example, people often confuse *desert* and *dessert*. How can you remember that *dessert* is the food we eat at the end of the meal? Link it to *strawberry shortcake*. Both *dessert* and *strawberry shortcake* have two *s's*.

Write It.

Back in the old days, some teachers made tardy students write "I will not be late!" over and over. You can bet the students remembered to be on time. Here's an easier way to use this memory aid: Write out the word, and then trace it with your finger. You can also write it over and over. Both methods work very well, especially when you have to memorize words for spelling and vocabulary tests.

Group It.

Grouping items together also helps you remember them. Groups of three-to-four work best. Maybe that's why we put a comma after every set of three numbers. Try it now. Group these numbers to help you remember them:

NOT GROUPED: 718046381
GROUPED: 718,046,381

Say It.

Just repeating the information aloud will help you memorize it.

Review It.

To fix the information in your mind, you have to review it. Go over the information each day for 5-10 minutes. This will help the information stay in your memory.

Work to Your Strengths

We're all different, so it's no surprise that we all learn in different ways. Figuring out how you learn best can help you make the most of your study time. It can help make learning easier and more fun, too. Clearly, this helps you do your best on standardized tests.

Researchers believe there are seven different learning styles. Everyone has at least one strong learning style, but some people have more than one that they can tap into. **Fill out the worksheet below to identify your learning style.** **Check each column that describes you.**

LEARNING STYLE	DESCRIPTION
auditory-musical	I learn best by setting information to music, tunes, and jingles; studying with quiet music in the background; and having someone read to me.
interpersonal	I learn best by working in groups or studying with a partner.
intrapersonal	I learn best by studying alone.
kinesthetic	I learn best by acting out concepts as I read and review them and by moving around as I study.
linguistic	I learn best by reading information, using color-coded notes/highlighted notes, and using flash cards and other visual aids.
logical-mathematical	I learn best by trying new ways of solving problems, by breaking big tasks into smaller steps, and by looking for the reasons behind the information.
spatial	I learn best by building models, sketching abstract concepts to make them specific; looking at pictures, illustrations, charts, and diagrams in books; and drawing my own pictures and charts.

what's your style?

DOES IT DESCRIBE ME?

DIFFERENT LEARNING STYLES

Choose the one or two learning styles that best describe you. Write them here:

USE YOUR LEARNING STYLE

How can you use this information to do better on standardized tests? First, identify your strongest learning styles. If you're not sure, try different methods until you find the ones that work best for you. Then adapt how you study to that learning style. For example, if you are an interpersonal learner, set up a study group of classmates who are also interpersonal learners. Study on your own, but then study with your group. This will help you review and memorize the facts, statistics, and details you need to earn a high score.

Next, match different methods to different classes. For instance, you might learn science most easily by building models and studying the illustrations and diagrams in books. This means that you are a spatial learner in science. But you might learn math best by setting the formulas to music or rhymes. This suggests that you are an auditory-musical learner when it comes to math.

Deal with Learning Disabilities

Some students follow all the study methods described in this book. They work hard. They pay attention. But they still have trouble learning. *Does this describe you?*

Everyone has problems learning some of the time. But if you find that you have trouble learning nearly all the time, you may have a learning disability (also called "learning differences"). Always consult with an expert if you suspect that you have a learning disability.

THE AMERICANS WITH DISABILITIES ACT

The Americans with Disabilities Act (ADA) of 1990 guarantees that people who have disabilities receive fair and equal access to all public services. This includes school. All schools that get money from the federal government must help students who have disabilities. All public schools get federal money. Some private schools do, too. Consult with an expert to learn more about learning disabilities and the law.

TWO THINGS MUST HAPPEN FOR YOU TO GET HELP:

1. *You must be classified as learning disabled.*

2. *You must ask for the help.*

It is your responsibility to give the school the papers that say you have a learning disability. The school will then create an Individualized Educational Plan (IEP) for you. The Plan will describe the help you can get. For example, if you have trouble writing, you might be able to use a tape recorder. You might get an aide to write for you. If you have trouble focusing, you might be given longer to finish a test.

FAMOUS PEOPLE WITH LEARNING DISABILITIES

Having a learning disability doesn't stand in the way of great success. Below is a list of famous people who have a learning disability. *Can you name each person's outstanding achievements?*

Winston Churchill
Charles Darwin
Julius Caesar
Tom Cruise
Walt Disney
Cher
Leonardo da Vinci
Michelangelo
George Washington
Lewis Carroll
Mark Twain
Whoopi Goldberg

In this chapter, you've learned the importance of memorizing. You've also learned how to use your learning style to make it easier for you to prepare for success on standardized tests. **Dealing with a possible learning disability is just another way to help you reach for the gold—and get it!**

Words help us understand other people and express our own opinions. If you know how to use words accurately, you'll do better on standardized reading and vocabulary tests. In this chapter, you'll have fun learning new words.

Build
Your Vocabulary
for Standardized Tests

know the vocabulary!

Sample Test

DIRECTIONS:
Each sentence below is missing one word. Under each sentence are possible answers. *Choose the answer that best completes each sentence. Fill in the circle of your answer.*

1. *Scientists believe that whales act _____, working together to ensure the safety of the pod.*

Ⓐ strangely
Ⓑ kindly
Ⓒ politely
Ⓓ courteously
Ⓔ cooperatively

2. *A decision made before all the evidence is available is best called _____.*

Ⓐ intelligent
Ⓑ premature
Ⓒ shrewd
Ⓓ prudent
Ⓔ judicious

DIRECTIONS:
Read the poem.
Then answer the questions that follow.

JAMES MCINTYRE *(1827-1906)*
Nova Scotia

1 *If you are sulky, Nova Scotia,*
2 *We'll gladly let you float away*
3 *From out our Confederation;*
4 *You sicken us with silly agitation.*
5 *If any more our patience you do tax*
6 *We'll let you go to Halifax.*

3. *The word sulky in line 1 most nearly means*

Ⓐ friendly
Ⓑ sociable
Ⓒ grouchy
Ⓓ weary
Ⓔ overcrowded

4. *Which is the best synonym for the word agitation in line 4?*

Ⓐ trouble
Ⓑ taxes
Ⓒ speeches
Ⓓ people
Ⓔ ideas

ANSWERS: **1.** E, **2.** B, **3.** C, **4.** A

Hints for Doing Your Best on Standardized Vocabulary Tests

As with every other test you take, knowing how to take a standardized vocabulary test can make a big difference in the outcome. Start with these hints:

1. *Read all the directions.* Be sure you understand the directions before you start the actual test. For example, what are you asked to do? Circle words? Bubble in answers?

2. *Underline key words.* The **stem** is the question itself. As you read the stem, look for the key word **synonym** (a word that means the same) or **antonym** (a word that means the opposite). The phrases w*hich is the best synonym for, most nearly means,* or *most closely means,* for instance, show that you're looking for a synonym.

3. *Look for transitions.* Transitions are words that link parts of a sentence. Some common transitions are **but**, **although**, **however**, **yet**, **even though**, **for**, **because**, **since**. These words show the relationship between the two parts of the sentence. The transitions *but, although, however, yet* indicate the two parts of the sentence will contrast each other. The second part will be the opposite of the first part. The transitions *for, because, since* show that the second part of the sentence will explain the first part.

4. *Look for negatives.* These are the words **no** and **not**. Usually, they show that you are looking for a word that is the opposite.

5. *Make predictions.* Read the sentence. Think about what it means before you look at the choices. Fill in the word in your mind. Then look for the closest word among the choices.

6. *Answer two-blank questions one blank at a time.* Some fill-in-the-blank vocabulary test questions will have one blank; a few will have two. When you're working on questions with two blanks, start with the first blank. If you can eliminate the first word in a pair, you can eliminate the entire choice.

7. *Use logic.* It's true that sentence-completion questions depend on your knowing the words, but you can—and should—use the logic in the sentence. Once you make your choice, read over the sentence to make sure it makes sense. If it doesn't, choose again.

8. *Keep working.* If you get stuck on a question, leave it and move on. You may get a clue to it later in the test. If not, you don't want to lose too much time on one test item.

9. *Guess.* Should you guess? Yes—if there's no penalty. No matter what, always eliminate some choices first. This helps increase the odds that you'll chose the correct answer.

10. *Check your work.* Try to leave enough time to check your answers. If you can't check them all, check the ones that count the most.

All these hints can help you do your best on standardized reading and vocabulary tests, but above all, **you have to know the vocabulary!** Some suggestions for learning vocabulary are on the following pages.

Make Word Cards

One of the best ways to make a word your own is by going over it again and again. Buy a stack of 3 x 5 index cards. As you read in class and on your own, write each test-worthy word on the front of an index card, one word per card. How can you tell what words to learn? Use vocabulary from practice tests. Then write the definition on the back. Here's a sample:

Study the cards every chance you get. Take them with you on the school bus, to the dentist's office, and in the car on the way to soccer practice. Sneak a peek. Rotate the cards so you learn many different words. The more words you study, the faster your vocabulary will increase.

flashy

gaudy

Use Context Clues

To figure out the meaning of an unfamiliar word, use context clues based on what you already know and the details in the paragraph. Here's an example:

Just before midnight on April 14, 1912, one of the most dramatic and famous of all *maritime* disasters occurred, the sinking of the *Titanic*. The *Titanic* was the most luxurious ship afloat at the time, with its beautifully decorated staterooms, glittering crystal chandeliers, and elaborate food service.

How can you figure out that **maritime** *must mean "related to the sea, nautical"?*
Use context clues:
WHAT YOU ALREADY KNOW
The *Titanic* was an ocean liner.
SENTENCE DETAILS
"The *Titanic* was the most luxurious ship afloat..."

Try it now.
Define **futile** *as it is used in this passage:*
The "unsinkable" *Titanic* vanished under the water at 2:20 AM, April 15. There were about 2,200 passengers aboard, and all but 678 died. The tragedy was made even worse by the crew's *futile* rescue attempts. Since there were not enough lifeboats, hundreds of people died who could have survived.

Discover Word Origins

Exploring the history of words can help you learn many useful everyday words. Knowing a word's history makes it easier to remember, too. For instance:

* **mentor:** In the epic poem *The Odyssey*, Mentor is Odysseus's friend. He also tutors Odysseus's son Telemachus. Today, the term *mentor* means "trusted teacher or guide."
* **denims:** One of the words we use for blue jeans comes from "Serge di Nimes," the city in France where the stiff blue fabric was made.
* **jeans:** The word for a specific kind of pants is from the city where its cloth was made—Genoa, Italy. From *Genoa* came *jene*; from *jene*, *jeans*

Learn Synonyms and Antonyms

As you read earlier in this chapter, **synonyms** are words that are nearly the same in meaning as other words. **Antonyms** are words that are opposites. Synonyms and antonyms often appear on standardized tests because you're being tested on your knowledge of shades of meaning. Also, knowing synonyms and antonyms helps you do better on the writing part of standardized tests. That's because you'll express yourself with greater accuracy and clarity. Try it now.

Complete the following chart by writing at least one synonym and antonym for each word. Then see how many more synonyms and antonyms you can brainstorm.

WORD	SYNONYM	ANTONYM
1. *adapt*		
2. *authentic*		
3. *chronic*		
4. *conquer*		
5. *frustrate*		
6. *indulge*		
7. *naive*		
8. *punish*		
9. *relinquish*		
10. *sullen*		

POSSIBLE ANSWERS

SYNONYMS:

1. *adapt* — adjust, accustom, accommodate
2. *authentic* — genuine, real, legitimate
3. *chronic* — habitual, ongoing, constant
4. *conquer* — defeat, vanquish, overwhelm
5. *frustrate* — baffle, beat, disappoint
6. *indulge* — tolerate, humor, allow, permit
7. *naive* — innocent
8. *punish* — discipline, correct, penalize
9. *relinquish* — quit, renounce, abandon, resign
10. *sullen* — irritable, morose, moody

ANTONYMS:

1. *adapt* — dislocate, disarrange
2. *authentic* — fake, counterfeit, bogus, imitation
3. *chronic* — one time, single
4. *conquer* — surrender, yield, forfeit, give up
5. *frustrate* — facilitate, encourage
6. *indulge* — prohibit, deter, restrain, enjoin
7. *naive* — worldly, suave
8. *punish* — reward, compensate
9. *relinquish* — perpetuate, keep
10. *sullen* — cheerful, jolly, blithe, happy

Distinguish Between Easily Confused Words.

English has many words that are easily confused. **Homonyms** are words with the same spelling and pronunciations but different meanings, such as as *bore/bore*, *lay/lay*, *lie/lie*. **Homophones/ homographs** are words with the same pronunciation but different spellings and meanings, such as *heir/air*, *weather/ whether*, *hear/here*. Being able to tell the difference between these words is important for your success on standardized tests in many ways.

WORD	DEFINITION	EXAMPLE
accept *except*	take leave out	*Accept my thanks.* *Everyone except him.*
affect *effect*	influence result	*This affects your ear.* *The effect of the law.*
already *all ready*	before prepared	*Lou already left.* *She was all ready to go.*
all together *altogether*	everyone at once completely	*They yell all together.* *It was altogether wrong.*
bare *bear*	uncovered animal endured	*The window was bare.* *The bear growled.* *How do you bear the noise?*
brake *break*	stop destroy	*Use the car's brake.* *Don't break the dish!*
capital *Capitol*	government seat where the US legislature meets	*Visit the capital.* *Congress meets in the Capitol.*
conscience *conscious*	morally right awake	*Listen to your conscience.* *She was conscious during surgery.*
desert *dessert*	leave behind arid region sweet	*Never desert a sinking ship.* *Camels travel in the desert.* *I love a rich dessert.*

First, it ensures that you understand what you're reading. Further, some answer choices include homophones and homographs. Finally, being able to distinguish between confusing word pairs helps you express yourself clearly and precisely on the writing section of standardized tests. Then you won't confuse the scorer.

WORD	DEFINITION	EXAMPLE
lay	put down	PRESENT: *The cat lies down.* PAST: *The cat lay down.* FUTURE: *The cat will lie down.* PERFECT: *The cat has lain down.*
lie	be flat	PRESENT: *Lay your cards down.* PAST: *He laid the cards down.* FUTURE: *He will lay his cards down.* PERFECT: *She has laid her cards down*
loose *lose*	not fastened misplace	*The clasp is loose.* *Jani might lose the necklace.*
principal *principle*	main head of a school rule	*The principal road is Main St.* *Dr. Richie is the principal.* *You know the principles of electronics.*
than *then*	comparison at that time	Kansas is bigger than Rhode Island. The state was then very rainy.
their *there* *they're*	belonging to them place they are (contraction)	It is their book. Put it there. They're good friends.
weather *whether*	atmospheric conditions if	We heard the weather forecast. Whether or not you agree.

Use Word Parts.

Many big words can be divided into parts that you can figure out easily. If you can define the parts, then you can often figure out the whole word. There are three main word parts to know: **prefixes**, **suffixes**, and **roots**.

∗ A **prefix** is letter or a group of letters at the beginning of a word that changes its meaning.
∗ A **suffix** is letter or a group of letters at the end of a word that changes its meaning.
∗ A **root** is a base or stem form of many words.

Try it now with the word *hydropower*. Hydro means "*water.*" *Power* means "*energy.*" What do you think *hydropower* means? It's power generated from water. **Now, complete the chart below to see how many more words you can decode by knowing their parts.**

WORD	PREFIX	ROOT	SUFFIX
1. *atypical*	a- = not	typical = average	none
2. *asteroid*	aster- = star	oid = round	none
3. *bibliophile*	biblio- = book	phile = lover	none
4. *hydrophobia*	hydro- = water	phobia = fear	none
5. *polychromatic*	poly- = many	chrom = color	-ic = like
6. *cardiac*	none	cardio = heart	-iac = like
7. *Romanesque*	none	Roman	-esque = resembling
8. *curvaceous*	none	curve	-aceous = having
9. *perilous*	none	peril = danger	-ous = full of
10. *thermometer*	therm- = temperature	meter = measuring device	-ate = to make

Even if you can't define a word exactly, recognizing the root will still give you a general idea of the word's meaning.

Using a dictionary helps you check what a word means and how it is used, but dictionaries give us a lot more than a list of words and their meanings. Dictionaries also give a word's part of speech and its pronunciation, which helps you use it correctly. Many dictionaries give you a word's origin, which helps you remember it. In addition, some dictionaries provide synonyms. Best of all, looking up a word helps you remember it, which comes in handy at test time.

MEANING

ANSWERS:

1. **atypical** not average; 2. **asteroid** star-like body;
3. **bibliophile** book collector; 4. **hydrophobia** fear of water;
5. **polychromatic** many colored; 6. **cardiac** having to do with the heart;
7. **Romanesque** like the Romans; 8. **curvaceous** having curves or twists;
9. **perilous** full of danger; 10. **thermometer** device for measuring temperature

Use the New Words!

Using a word often in conversation and writing (when it fits, of course!) will help you make it part of your everyday vocabulary. You don't have to be stuffy about it, but using just the right word helps you say what you want clearly. This makes it easier for people to communicate clearly.

use it!

Play Word Games.

Here's a fun way to learn new words: Play games. Word games help you learn, remember, and use new words. Scrabble, Boggle, and crossword puzzles are a lot of fun.

The more often you use a word, the more likely you are to remember it during a test.

Self Test

DIRECTIONS:

Each sentence below is missing one word. Under each sentence are possible answers. Choose the answer that best completes each sentence. Fill in the circle of your answer.

1. *Even in zoos, wild animals are often so _____ that it's difficult to get a clear look at them.*

Ⓐ careless
Ⓑ wary
Ⓒ huge
Ⓓ abundant
Ⓔ plentiful

2. *Although they have _____ backgrounds, Harry and Marielle found they had much in common.*

Ⓐ identical
Ⓑ unremarkable
Ⓒ dissimilar
Ⓓ eccentric
Ⓔ fine

3. *The Renaissance was a new beginning, a _____ of literature, architecture, and painting.*

Ⓐ regurgitation
Ⓑ revolt
Ⓒ riot
Ⓓ renewal
Ⓔ ridicule

4. *A(n) _____ is not concerned with the label put on a plan, but whether or not the plan will be a success.*

Ⓐ beginner
Ⓑ politician
Ⓒ fanatic
Ⓓ idealist
Ⓔ realist

5. *The _____ discovery was _____ even to the successful inventor, who was proud of it all her life.*

Ⓐ remarkable… exceptional
Ⓑ forgettable…unique
Ⓒ astonishing… unexceptional
Ⓓ unexciting …spectacular
Ⓔ wonderful…offensive

ANSWERS: 1. B, 2. C, 3. D, 4. E, 5. A

CHAPTER 4: **Build Your Vocabulary for Standardized Tests**

CHAPTER 5

Review Your Math Skills

There are so many standardized math tests! First of all, many major national standardized tests contain math sections. As you learned earlier in this book, you'll likely take your PSAT during middle school. This is a standardized test that has math sections and verbal sections. You take this test to compete for scholarships and to help you prepare for your college entrance exam, the SAT. If you want to attend a private high school, you'll most likely have to take the Independent School Entrance Exam (ISEE). This is a three-hour multiple-choice test given to students in grades 5-12. The test measures math and verbal skills. Both these tests are administered by the Educational Testing Service.

There are also special national standardized math tests such as the *Algebra End-of-Course Assessment.* Administered by the Educational Testing Service, the *Algebra End-of-Course Assessment* is designed to help middle school and high school teachers jointly plan and adjust teaching strategies. It's a multiple choice test that measures what you know about algebra.

Why so many standardized math tests?

It's because educators recognize the importance of math no matter what career you choose. So let's plunge right in with some suggestions for mastering standardized math tests.

Hints for Doing Your Best on Standardized Math Tests

As with every other test you take, knowing how to take a standardized math test matters. Start with these hints:

1. *Read all the directions.*
For example, you may be able to use a calculator or you may have to show all your work. Be sure you understand the directions before you start the actual test.

2. *Read the entire math problem first.*
Read each math problem all the way through before you begin to solve it. If you skim the problem, you may misunderstand what you need to do.

3. *Underline key words.* Look for key words that will tell you what you need to do, such as **add**, **subtract**, **multiply**, and **divide**.

4. *Draw a picture.* Even though you may be able to see the problem in your head, drawing a diagram helps you check your ideas. It helps you see the problem from different angles, too. Unless you are told otherwise, draw your picture in the test book or on scrap paper.

5. *Check units of measurement.*
Be sure that you are working in the same units of measurement when you perform calculations. For instance, if a problem involves inches and feet, put all your numbers in the same unit of measure, such as inches.

stay calm

6. *Show all your work, if asked.*
If you are asked to show your work, show it *all.* Even show the work that you did on your calculator. Include diagrams, calculations, and explanations. Write in complete sentences because it helps the scorer understand what you did.

7. *Check your logic.* Make sure that your answer makes sense. For example, say a question asks you to find the number of feet in a diagram. Your answer comes out to be a negative number. You know that the answer can't be correct.

8. *Estimate.* Estimating is rounding the numbers. Estimating helps you decide if your answer makes sense. Round the numbers to the highest (or lowest, if you're working with small decimals) place. Then do the easier calculations with those numbers. If your final answer comes out close to your estimated answer, it's likely to be correct.

9. *Work carefully and stay cool.*
Tests are pressure situations. Still, work slowly and carefully. Try not to get flustered. Focus on what you DO know, not on what you do not know. You know a great deal of math already. By the end of this chapter, you'll have reviewed a lot of it.

10. *Recognize extra information.* Don't feel that you must use every number in a problem. That's because some mathematics problems have extra information. These questions are testing your ability to recognize what information you need, as well as your math skills.

11. *Keep working.* If you get stuck on a problem, leave it and move on. You may get a clue to it later in the test. If not, you don't want to lose too much time on one problem.

12. *Solve for other information.*
You may have to solve for additional information before you get the answer. These two-step problems test your ability to perform more than one step in a problem.

13. *Check your work.* Try to leave enough time to check your answers. If you can't check them all, check the ones that count the most. For example, say that some questions count 1 point each. Other questions count 10 points each. If you are running out of time, check the questions that count 10 points each.

14. *Guess.* Should you guess? Yes, if there is no penalty. In any case, always try to eliminate some choices first. This helps increase the odds that you will choose the correct answer.

Below is a review of basic math.
This is the math you are expected to know in middle school.
You learned some of it in elementary school.
The rest you learned in middle school.

Types of Numbers

Counting Numbers:
All numbers that don't have decimals or fractions as part of them and are greater than zero, all the way to infinity. **EXAMPLE:** 1, 2, 3, 4…

Whole Numbers:
All of the counting numbers, including zero.
EXAMPLE: 0, 1, 2, 3…

Integers:
All positive and negative whole numbers.
EXAMPLE: 1, 18, -3, 0.

Real Numbers:
All positive and negative numbers, including those that have decimal places or fractions.
EXAMPLE: 6.31, 7 ¾, -½

Cardinal Numbers:
Numbers that tell amounts. Any whole number can be a cardinal number.
EXAMPLE: There are 4 socks in a package, and 10 packages for sale.

Ordinal Numbers:
Numbers that tell order.
EXAMPLE: 1st, 2nd and 3rd person to buy concert tickets.

Ordering Numbers

You can compare numbers to one another using symbols.
If two numbers are the same, use the **equals** (=) sign.
EXAMPLE: $2 + 2 = 4$ "Two plus two *equals* four."

If the numbers are different, use the symbols
less than (<) or **greater than** (>).
The arrow points towards the smaller number.
EXAMPLES:
$10 < 15$ "Ten is *less than* fifteen."
$7 > 4$ "Seven is greater than four."

Place Value

Our math system uses **base ten**, which means we write out numbers using a combination of ten digits: 0, 1, 2, 3, 4, 5, 6, 7, 8, and 9.

When you write a number greater than 9, you move up into the next **place**. 10 means "1 ten and 0 ones." 56 means "5 tens and 6 ones." **The following chart shows the order of the places.**

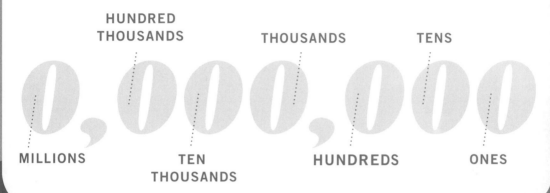

HUNDRED THOUSANDS

THOUSANDS

TENS

MILLIONS

TEN THOUSANDS

HUNDREDS

ONES

Self Test

Identify each item as a counting number, whole number, integer, or real number. Say everything that applies.

1. 12

2. –9

3. 0

Put =, <, or > in the space to make the equation true.

4. 5 ____ 19

5. 4 ____ 1

ANSWERS
1. counting, whole, integer, and real
2. integer and real
3. whole, integer, and real
4. 5 < 19
5. 4 > 1

Arithmetic with Whole Numbers

ADDITION

First, line up the digits so that similar places are in columns. Then add each column. Remember to carry over ones to the next column.

EXAMPLE: *649,041 + 34,790*

```
  6 4 9 0 4 1
+   3 4 7 9 0
─────────────


    1     1
  6 4 9 0 4 1
+   3 4 7 9 0
─────────────
  6 8 3 8 3 1
```

SUBTRACTION

Set this up the same way as addition. Remember that you can "borrow" ten from the next place.

EXAMPLE: *508,567 − 14,695*

```
  5 0 8 5 6 7
-   1 4 6 9 5
─────────────


  4   7 4
  5 0 8 5 6 7
-   1 4 6 9 5
─────────────
  4 9 3 8 7 2
```

MULTIPLICATION

Multiply each place in turn, and remember to bring down a zero with each new line. Then add all of the partial products. A **_partial product_** is a product obtained by multiplying a multiplicand by one digit of a multiplier having more than one digit.

EXAMPLE: _428 x 36_

```
    4 2 8
  x   3 6
  ─────────
```

FIRST PARTIAL PRODUCT:

```
  2 1 4
    4 2 8
  x   3 6
  ─────────
  2 5 6 8
```

SECOND PARTIAL PRODUCT:

```
        2
    4 2 8
  x   3 6
  ─────────
    2 5 6 8
  1 2 8 4 0
```

THEN ADD:

```
    2 5 6 8
+ 1 2 8 4 0
─────────────
  1 5 4 0 8
```

DIVISION

Set up the problem as illustrated in the example. Divide each part of the number and bring down the remainder. The **_remainder_** is the final undivided part that is less than the divisor. (R= remainder.)

EXAMPLE: _993 ÷ 12_

```
        ┌─────────
  1 2   │ 9 9 3
```

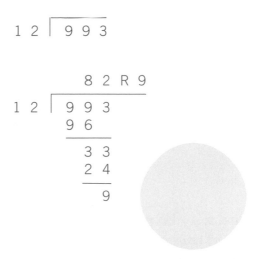

```
              8 2 R 9
        ┌─────────────
  1 2   │ 9 9 3
          9 6
          ─────
            3 3
            2 4
            ─────
              9
```

Order of Operations

This is the order in which you work out the various operations in a problem. The order is: Parentheses, Exponents, Multiply and Divide, Addition and Subtraction.

STEP #1
Do everything inside parentheses (starting with the innermost parentheses, if there are several sets).

STEP #2
Solve all of the exponents.

STEP #3
Do all of the multiplication and division (from left to right).

STEP #4
Do all of the addition and subtraction (from left to right).

A good way to remember the order of operations is the phrase, "Please Excuse My Dear Aunt Sally." The first letter of each word stands for the order of operations:

Please **[Parentheses]**
Excuse **[Exponents]**
My **[Multiply]**
Dear **[Divide]**
Aunt **[Addition]**
Sally **[Subtraction]**.

EXAMPLES:
$5 + (12 \div 6) = 5 + 2 = 7$
$10 \times (4 - 2) = 10 \times 2 = 20$

Self Test

1. $1 + 2 \times 3 + 4 - 5 =$ ....

2. $(1 + 2) \times 3 + (4 - 5) =$ ....

3. $3 + 4^2 =$ ....

ANSWERS
1. 6, **2.** 8, **3.** 19

Rounding

To round a number to a specific place, look to the place directly to the right of it (that is, the next lowest place). *If that digit is five or greater, round up. If it's four or less, round down.* When you round up, add one to the digit in the specified place. Change all the digits to the right of it to zeroes. When you round down, leave the specified digit as is. Change the lower places to zeroes.

EXAMPLE:
Round 663,465 to the nearest thousand. 3 is in the thousands place, and 4 is in the place directly to the right of it (the hundreds place). Since 4 is less than 5, we round down. The answer is 663,000.

don't be a square!

Self Test

1. *Round 9,475 to the nearest ten* ....

2. *Round 48,799 to the nearest thousand* ....

3. *Round 71,146 to the nearest hundred* ....

ANSWERS
1. 9,480 **2.** 49,000 **3.** 71,100

Arithmetic with Integers

Adding a negative number is the same as subtracting a positive one. When adding integers, remember that if the signs are the same, you're getting further from zero, and if they're different, you're getting closer.

If the signs are the same, add the numbers and use the same sign. If the signs are different, subtract the numbers and take the sign of the larger one.

EXAMPLE: 9 + -3 = 6

When you **subtract** integers, change the sign of the number being subtracted, and then add.

EXAMPLE:
18 – -6 = 18 + 6 = 24

When you **multiply** and **divide** integers, everything works the same as with whole numbers — until the end. Then, if the two integers you multiplied had the same sign (both positive or both negative), the answer is positive. If they have different signs (one positive and one negative) the answer is negative. It is exactly the same when you divide integers.

EXAMPLES:
-6 x 6 = -36
-2 x -7 = 14

Self Test

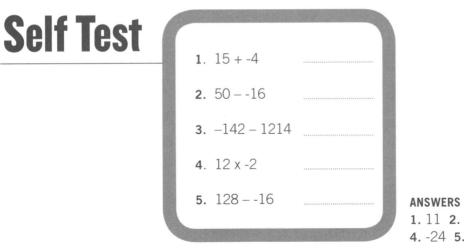

1. 15 + -4 ....

2. 50 – -16 ....

3. –142 – 1214 ....

4. 12 x -2 ....

5. 128 – -16 ....

ANSWERS
1. 11 **2.** 66 **3.** -1356
4. -24 **5.** 112

Rules of Divisibility

If a number is **divisible** by another, you can divide it evenly with no remainder—that is, the divisor is one of the factors. Remember the following rules:

* *Every even number is divisible by 2.*

* *Add up the digits: If the sum is divisible by 3, the number is divisible by 3. If the sum is divisible by 9, the number is divisible by 9.* **EXAMPLE:** Try this rule with 81. 8 + 1 = 9. 9 is divisible by 3 and 9. This means that 81 is divisible by 3 and 9.

* *If a number is divisible by both 2 and 3, it is also divisible by 6.*

* *If the last digit is 0 or 5, the number is divisible by 5. If the last digit is 0, the number is divisible by 10.*

* *If the last two digits are divisible by 4, the number is divisible by 4. If the last three digits are divisible by 8, the number is divisible by 8.* **EXAMPLE:** What are the last two digits of 316? 16. Is 16 divisible by 4? Yes. That means 316 is divisible by 4.

Percentages

Percentages are another way of writing numbers smaller than one. A number followed by the percent sign is expressed in hundredths. To change a decimal into a percentage, move the decimal point two places to the right. To change a percentage into a decimal, move the decimal point two places to the left.

EXAMPLES:
0.72 = 72%
93.45% = 0.9345

Self Test

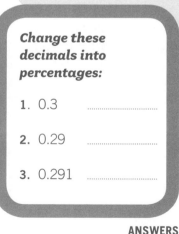

Change these decimals into percentages:

1. 0.3 ....

2. 0.29 ....

3. 0.291 ....

ANSWERS
1. 30% **2.** 29% **3.** 29.1%

Finding a Percentage of a Number

To find any percentage of a number, change the percentage into a decimal and multiply.

EXAMPLE: *What is 17% of 40?*
0.17 x 40 = 6.8

Fractions

Fractions are another way of expressing numbers between zero and one. A fraction has two parts, the **numerator** and the **denominator**. The numerator is how many pieces you have. The denominator is how many pieces there are all together.

EXAMPLE:

$\frac{7}{10}$ Numerator

    Denominator

In this example, ten pieces make up the whole and you have seven of them.

IMPROPER FRACTIONS AND MIXED NUMBERS

In an improper fraction, the numerator is greater than the denominator. In a mixed number, you write both a whole number part and a fraction part.

EXAMPLES: $\frac{3}{2}$ is an improper fraction.

3 is greater than 2, so the entire expression is greater than 1. This is said as, "Three halves" or "Three over two."

$2\frac{1}{2}$ is a mixed number.
It is said as "Two and one half."

EQUIVALENT FRACTIONS

Fractions that are equal are **equivalent**. You can change any fraction into an equivalent one by multiplying (or dividing) the numerator and denominator by the same number.

COMPARING FRACTIONS

You can find out if two fractions are equivalent by **cross-multiplying**. Multiply the numerator of each fraction by the denominator of the other fraction, and compare those two numbers.

EXAMPLE:

Compare $\frac{3}{8}, \frac{7}{11}$

3 x 11 = 33, 8 x 7 = 56

33 < 56, so $\frac{3}{8} < \frac{7}{11}$

SIMPLEST TERMS

To write a fraction into simplest terms, find the greatest common factor (GCF) of the numerator and denominator and divide both by it. If the GCF is 1, then the fraction is already in lowest terms.

EXAMPLE:

Put $\frac{10}{25}$ into simplest terms.

Factors of 10 are 1, 2, 5, 10
Factors of 25 are 1, 5, 25

The greatest common factor is 5, so

$$\frac{(10 \div 5)}{(25 \div 5)} = \frac{2}{5}$$

EXAMPLE:

$$4\frac{2}{7} = \frac{(4 \times 7) + 2}{7} = \frac{30}{7}$$

ARITHMETIC WITH FRACTIONS
First change all the mixed numbers into improper fractions.

To add and subtract fractions, you must have a **common denominator**: the denominators of the two fractions must be the same. To find a common denominator, change the fractions into equivalent fractions. A good common denominator is the Least Common Multiple of the two denominators. Then multiply the top and bottom of each fraction by the same number to get equivalent fractions with that denominator.

EXAMPLE:

$$\frac{2}{5} + \frac{1}{4}$$

MULTIPLES OF 5: 5, 10, 15, 20, 25
MULTIPLES OF 4: 4, 8, 12, 16, 20, 24
The LCM is 20.

$$\frac{(2 \times 4)}{(5 \times 4)} + \frac{(1 \times 5)}{(4 \times 5)} = \frac{8}{20} + \frac{5}{20} = \frac{13}{20}$$

To multiply fractions, multiply numerator times numerator, and denominator times denominator. To divide, take the **reciprocal** of the fraction you're dividing by, and then multiply.

To take the reciprocal of a fraction, flip it over. When you take the reciprocal of a whole number, it becomes $\frac{1}{\text{number}}$. Any number times its reciprocal equals 1.

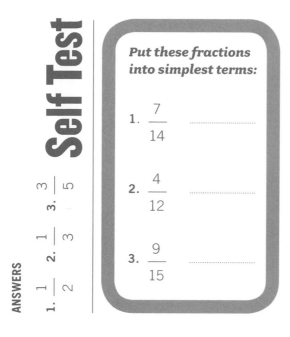

Self Test

Put these fractions into simplest terms:

1. $\frac{7}{14}$ ....

2. $\frac{4}{12}$ ....

3. $\frac{9}{15}$ ....

ANSWERS

1. $\frac{1}{2}$ 2. $\frac{1}{3}$ 3. $\frac{3}{5}$

CHANGING FRACTIONS TO MIXED NUMBERS
To change an improper fraction into a mixed number, divide the numerator by the denominator. The answer becomes the whole-number part. The remainder is left as a fraction.

EXAMPLE:

Change $\frac{22}{5}$ into a mixed number.

$22 \div 5 = 4$ Remainder $2 = 4\frac{2}{5}$

To change a mixed number into an improper fraction, multiply the denominator by the whole number, and add that to the numerator.

Algebra: Solving Equations

Algebra is math using **variables**, letters that stand in for numbers you don't know. The letter **x** is a common variable. When you solve an **algebraic equation** (an equation that has a variable in it), you're trying to find out what the variable equals.

Solve simple algebraic equations with this three-step process:

STEP #1
Combine like terms.

STEP #2
Add or subtract both sides.

STEP #3
Multiply or divide both sides.

EXAMPLE:
2x + 9x = 33
Combine 2x and 9x by adding the numerical part.
2x + 9x = 11x

With equations, both sides have to be equal. If you do something to one side, you have to do the same thing to the other side. With this sample equation, you divide both sides by 11 because you want to get x by itself. You use 11 here because that's the number in the equation and any number divided by itself is 1.

$11x = 33$

$$\frac{11x}{11} = \frac{33}{11}$$

$x = 3$

EXAMPLE:
$$\begin{array}{r} x - 5 = 9 \\ +5\ +5 \\ \hline x = 14 \end{array}$$

Self Test

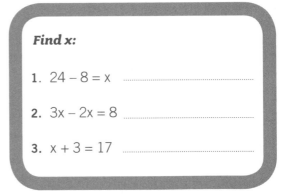

Find x:

1. 24 − 8 = x ....

2. 3x − 2x = 8 ....

3. x + 3 = 17 ....

ANSWERS
1. x = 16 **2.** x = 8 **3.** x = 14

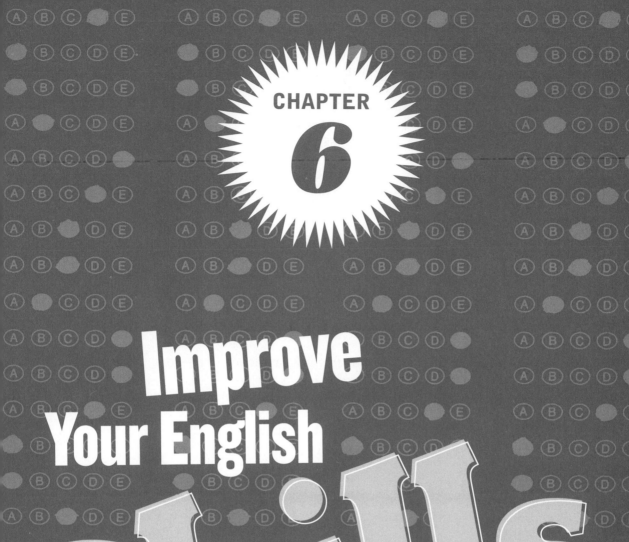

CHAPTER 6

Improve Your English Skills

Sample Test

Many standardized tests assess your ability to use your English skills. Sometimes you'll have multiple-choice tests. Other times, you'll have to write essays. You'll find both kinds of test items on standardized tests such as the PSAT and ACT. In all cases, you'll have to know the rules of Standard Written English.
What kinds of test questions can you expect?
Try the sample test below to find out.

DIRECTIONS: Read the passage. Some words and phrases are underlined.
Choose the answer that makes the sentence Standard Written English.
If the original version is correct, choose NO CHANGE.
Fill in the circle of your answer.

Nature's Fury

<u>During a thunderstorm lightning</u> bolts (which are hotter than the surface of the sun) flash
₁

across the sky. These streaks of electricity heat the air around them to 20,000 degrees

<u>Fahrenhiet</u> or more. <u>A lightning bolt's power lasts a fraction</u> of a <u>second, it</u> has enough
₂ ₃ ₄

power to light up all of Miami! Because the average thunderstorm is <u>more powerfuler</u> than
₅

an atomic bomb, injuries from these storms are common.

1.
Ⓐ During a thunderstorm, lightning
Ⓑ During a thunderstorm lightening
Ⓒ During a thunderstorm lightning,
Ⓓ NO CHANGE

2.
Ⓐ Fahrenhite
Ⓑ Fahrenheit
Ⓒ Fahrienhiet
Ⓓ NO CHANGE

3.
Ⓐ A lightning bolts' power lasts a fraction
Ⓑ A lightning bolts power last's a fraction
Ⓒ A lightning bolt's power last's a fraction
Ⓓ NO CHANGE

4.
Ⓐ second it
Ⓑ second but it
Ⓒ second, but it
Ⓓ NO CHANGE

5.
Ⓐ more powerful
Ⓑ most powerful
Ⓒ powerfuler
Ⓓ NO CHANGE

ANSWERS AND EXPLANATIONS: 1. A Use a comma after any introductory word or word group. **2. B** *Fahrenheit* is an exception to the "i before e" rule. **3. D** Use an apostrophe to show ownership. **4. C** *Run-ons* are two incorrectly joined sentences. You can correct a run-on by adding *and, but, or, for, yet, so*. Use a comma before the word *and, but, or, for, so, nor, yet* when it joins two sentences. **5. A** Use the comparative degree (*-er* or *more* form) to compare two things. Never use *-er* and *more* or *-est* and *most* together.

Now that you know what to expect on these standardized tests, let's review the skills you need to ace them.

Capitalization Review

* **Capitalize the first word in a sentence.**
  EXAMPLE: _Teachers_ assign group projects in middle school.

* **Capitalize proper nouns and proper adjectives. These words name a specific person, place, or thing.**
  EXAMPLE: _Louise_ ordered _Italian_ dressing on her salad.
  Louise PROPER NOUN
  Italian PROPER ADJECTIVE

* **Capitalize titles.**
  EXAMPLES:
  _Dr._ Wang
  Professor Viola
  _Mr._ Ruiz
  _Ms._ Gyana

* **Capitalize historical events, months, days, holidays, famous places, organizations, languages, and religious references.**
  EXAMPLES:
  World War I
  April
  Thanksgiving
  Eiffel Tower
  Boy Scouts
  German
  Tuesday
  the Lord

* **Capitalize the first word and all nouns in a letter's greeting. Capitalize the first word in a letter's closing.**
  EXAMPLES:
  Dear Elliott,
  Dear Mr. Hmong:
  Yours very truly,

To capitalize or not to capitalize, that is the question...

Apostrophes

★ *A **contraction** results when two words are combined by leaving out letters.*
Put an apostrophe where the letter or letters have been taken out.

EXAMPLES:

TWO WORDS	CONTRACTION
I will	I'll
he is	he's

Contractions and possessive pronouns are not the same. Study this chart:

CONTRACTION	MEANING	POSSESSIVE PRONOUN	MEANING
it's	it is	*its*	belonging to it
you're	you are	*your*	belonging to you
who's	who is	*whose*	belonging to who
they're	they are	*their*	belonging to them

★ *Use an apostrophe to show ownership.*
Add *s* to the end of singular nouns, whether or not they end in *s*.
EXAMPLES:
book of the girl = girl's book
test of Charles = Charles's test

Add *s* to the end of plural nouns. If they already end in *s*, add an apostrophe only.
EXAMPLES:
game of children = children's game
roofs of the houses = houses' roofs

Periods

★ *Use a period at the end of a sentence and with abbreviations.*
EXAMPLES: We study every night.
<u>*Dr.*</u> Smith teaches John Jones <u>*Jr.*</u>
<u>*Dr.*</u> and <u>*Jr.*</u> **ABBREVIATIONS**

Question Marks

★ *Use a question mark at the end of a question.*
EXAMPLE: When is the test?

Exclamation Marks

* **Use an exclamation mark at the end of an *exclamatory sentence*.**
An exclamatory sentence is one in which strong emotion is shown.
EXAMPLE: Be sure to bring your calculator to the test!

Commas

* **Use commas between items in a list.**
EXAMPLE: The test will cover math, science, and social studies.

* **Use a comma after any introductory word or word group.**
EXAMPLE: *For the test,* we brought extra pencils.
For the test INTRODUCTORY WORDS

* **Use a comma before the words and, but, or, for, so, nor, and yet when they unite two sentences.**
EXAMPLE: *The test is on Thursday*, and *Nick is ready to take it.*
The test is on Thursday SENTENCE #1
Nick is ready to take it. SENTENCE #2

* **Use a comma after the greeting of a friendly letter and the closing of any letter.**
EXAMPLES:
Dear Mom,   Sincerely,   Best wishes,

* **Use a comma to separate a direct quotation from the speaker.**
EXAMPLE:
The teacher said, "Be sure to study."
COMMA BEFORE THE QUOTATION
"Be sure to study," the teacher said.
COMMA AFTER THE QUOTATION

* **Use commas with every three numbers, parts of an address, and with dates. Do not use a comma before the zip code.**
EXAMPLES:
2,000,192,081
68 Main Street, Long Beach, California 18651
May 2, 1006

Quotation Marks

* **Use quotation marks to set off a speaker's exact words.**
EXAMPLE: "Take notes on this page," said Mr. Nakema.

* **Use quotation marks to set off the titles of short works such as poems, essays, songs, short stories, and magazine articles.**
EXAMPLES:
"Annabel Lee"
"America the Beautiful"
"The Swimmer"

Semicolons

* **Use a semicolon to join complete sentences when the words and, but, or, for, so, nor, yet are not used.**
EXAMPLE: *Nancy works hard*; *she is a good student.*
Nancy works hard SENTENCE #1
She is a good student. SENTENCE #2

Spelling Review

✳ **The _ie_ or _ei_ rule:**
i before e except after c
or as sounded as a as in _neighbor_
and _weigh_

I BEFORE E	EXCEPT AFTER C	SOUNDED AS A	EXCEPTIONS TO THE RULE
achieve	conceit	neighbor	either
believe	ceiling	weigh	neither
siege	receive	freight	foreign
relief	conceive	reign	height
piece	deceit	sleigh	leisure
chief	deceive	vein	seize
fierce	perceive	weight	weird
fiend	receipt	beige	Fahrenheit
piece	receive	eight	protein
			fiery

✳ **The _-ful_ rule**
The sound _full_ at the end of a
word is spelled with only one _l_.
EXAMPLES:
careful
graceful

✳ **The _-ceed/-cede_ rule**
Only three verbs in English end in -_ceed_:
succeed, proceed, exceed.
All other verbs with that
sound end in -_cede_.
EXAMPLES:
precede
concede
secede
recede

✳ **_Q_ _is followed by_ _u_**
EXAMPLES:
quarter
quality
equality
quotation
quilt

pay
attention
to the
rules!

Plural nouns name more than one person, place, or thing. Follow these guidelines to form the plural of nouns:

ACTION	SINGULAR	PLURAL
*Add **s** to form the plural of most nouns.*	worm table pen shoes	worms tables pens shoes
*Add **es** if the noun ends in s, sh, ch, or x.*	class dish inch box	classes dishes inches boxes
*If the noun ends in **y** preceded by a **consonant**, change the y to i and add es.*	city lady	cities ladies
*If the noun ends in **y** preceded by a **vowel**, add s.*	essay monkey	essays monkeys
*Add **es** if the noun ends in o and is preceded by a **vowel**, add s.*	radio ratio	radios ratios
*Add **es** if the noun ends in o and is preceded by a **consonant**, the noun can take either s or es.*	potato hero zero	potatoes heroes zeros or zeroes
*Add **s** to most nouns ending in f.*	chief brief	chiefs briefs
EXCEPTION: *Sometimes you will need to change the f or fe to v and add es.*	self leaf knife	selves leaves knives
Some nouns change their spelling when they become plural.	child foot mouse	children feet mice
Some nouns have the same form and spelling whether they are singular or plural.	series deer sheep fish	series deer sheep fish

Parts of Speech

English words are divided into eight different parts of speech. They are *nouns, pronouns, verbs, adjectives, adverbs, conjunctions, interjections,* and *prepositions.*

Nouns *name a person, place, or thing.*
EXAMPLES:
Fido   suitcase   test   sunshine

Pronouns *are used in place of a noun.*
EXAMPLES: its   hers   I   who

Verbs *name an action or describe a state of being.*
EXAMPLES: run   feel   smell   to be

Adjectives *describe nouns and pronouns.* Adjectives answer the questions *What kind? How much? Which one? How many?*
EXAMPLES: beautiful   many   that   six

Adverbs *describe verbs, adjectives, or other adverbs.* Adverbs answer the questions *When? Where? How?* or *To what extent?* Many adverbs end in -ly.
EXAMPLES: yesterday   there   carefully   completely

Adjectives and Adverbs are words that describe.

MAKE CORRECT COMPARISONS WITH ADJECTIVES AND ADVERBS.

✻ *Use the* **comparative** *degree* (*-er* or *more* form) **to compare two things.**
EXAMPLE: This test is <u>*harder*</u> than that one. It's <u>*more complicated.*</u>

✻ *Use the* **superlative** *form* (*-est* or *most* form) **to compare more than two things.**
EXAMPLE: This is the <u>*easiest*</u> test I have ever taken.

Never use -er and more or -est and most together.

Conjunctions *connect words* or groups of words.
EXAMPLES:
and   but   or   not only…but also

Interjections *show strong emotion.*
EXAMPLES: Oh   Wow!   Look out!

Prepositions *link a noun or a pronoun to another word in the sentence.*
EXAMPLES: into   off   from   until

IDENTIFYING THE PART OF SPEECH
A word's part of speech depends on how it is used in a sentence.
EXAMPLES:
We caught three <u>*fish*</u>.   **NOUN**
We like to <u>*fish*</u>.   **VERB**

Sentences

Every sentence must have a noun (or pronoun) and a verb to be complete.

FRAGMENT MISSING A COMPLETE VERB: Teachers often giving homework.

FRAGMENT MISSING A SUBJECT: Often give homework.

SENTENCE: Teachers often give homework.

 A *sentence* must:
* *state a complete thought*
* *have a subject* (the noun or pronoun)
* *have a predicate* (the verb and other words)

EXAMPLE: Marta *took a test on Wednesday*.
SUBJECT   PREDICATE

SENTENCE TYPES : There are four types of sentences in English: *declarative, exclamatory, interrogative,* and *imperative*.

Declarative
sentences state an idea.
They end with a period.
EXAMPLE:
A report card shows your progress in class.

Exclamatory
sentences show strong emotions.
They end with an exclamation mark.
EXAMPLE:
What a good report card you received!

Interrogative
sentences ask a question.
They end with a question mark.
EXAMPLE:
How can you improve your grades?

Imperative
sentences give orders or directions.
They can end with a period or an exclamation mark.
EXAMPLE:
Study every night!

Run-ons are two incorrectly joined sentences.
EXAMPLE: The teacher gave a test it was a surprise.
You can correct a run-on sentence four ways:

Separate the run-on into two sentences.
EXAMPLE:
The teacher gave a test. It was a surprise.

Add and, but, or, for, yet, so.
EXAMPLE:
The teacher gave a test, but it was a surprise.

Add a subordinating conjunction.
EXAMPLE:
<u>When</u> the teacher gave a test, it was a surprise.
SUBORDINATING CONJUNCTION

Use a semicolon.
EXAMPLE:
The teacher gave a test; it was a surprise.

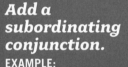

AVOID DOUBLE NEGATIVES
*A double **negative** is a statement that contains two negative describing words.* Use only one negative word to express a negative idea.

DOUBLE NEGATIVE:
I don't want no more extra help.
CORRECT:
I don't want any more extra help.
-or-
I don't want more extra help

Self Test

Timbuktu sat at the great bend of a <u>big river</u>, between the <u>citys of Niani and Gao.</u> <u>Over</u>
          1   2

<u>the years Timbuktu</u> grew from a group of tents to a great center for learning and trade.
          3

The city reached its peak during the <u>Songhai Empire it did not endure</u>. <u>Its' rulers</u> were
                                                          4   5

famous for their wisdom and leadership.

1.
Ⓐ Big River
Ⓑ Big river
Ⓒ big River
Ⓓ NO CHANGE

2.
Ⓐ cities of Niani and Gao.
Ⓑ cityes of Niani and Gao.
Ⓒ citys of niani and gao.
Ⓓ NO CHANGE

3.
Ⓐ Over the years: Timbuktu
Ⓑ Over the years, Timbuktu
Ⓒ Over the years; Timbuktu
Ⓓ NO CHANGE

4.
Ⓐ Songhai Empire, it did not endure
Ⓑ Songhai Empire so it did not endure
Ⓒ Songhai Empire, but it did not endure
Ⓓ NO CHANGE

5.
Ⓐ Its rulers
Ⓑ It rulers'
Ⓒ It's rulers
Ⓓ NO CHANGE

ANSWERS: 1. D, 2. A, 3. B, 4. C, 5. A

notes

As with all other tests, you can prepare for standardized writing tests. And as with those tests, preparation goes a long way to helping you earn a high score.

Write

Great Essays
for Standardized Tests

Writing at Home vs. Test Writing

"All writing is the same. It doesn't matter whether I write at home or in class," you say. Yes and no. All good writing shares the same qualities. It answers a question, has a clear method of organization, and provides vivid details. It also follows the rules of Standard Written English. **But writing at home is different from test writing.**

When you write at home, you have time to try different approaches, revise, and rewrite. But when you write on a test, you don't have the luxury of time. You're under pressure.

When you write at home, you can look up facts, details, and examples online or in books. But when you write on a test, you can only use the information you recall. You can't look up information on-line, in books, or in magazines.

When you write at home, you can ask friends or family to read your rough draft and offer suggestions. You have time for revisions. But when you write on a test, you can't ask anyone to read your draft. You may not have time for revisions. Your first copy will be your last copy. That's why you need a special approach to test writing.

Start by focusing on the type of writing you will be doing.

Understand the Writing Task

TYPE OF WRITING	DEFINITION
persuasive writing	convinces the reader about an issue
expository writing	explains something
narrative writing	tells a story
descriptive writing	uses images drawn from the five senses

On a standardized writing test, you'll be asked to persuade, explain, tell a story, or describe. The following chart summarizes the four kinds of test writing. The last column shows you some sample questions.

EXAMPLES	WAYS TO DEVELOP	SAMPLE TEST QUESTION
editorial letter to the editor	most-to-least important reasons least-to-most important reasons	*Argue that TV does or does not have educational value.* *Should students be allowed to have cell phones in school? Why or why not?*
textbook encyclopedia directions	compare/contrast definition problem/solution example classify/divide cause and effect classification	*How will the Internet change life in the 21st century?* *Explain how disappointments can have a positive side.*
short story novel	chronological (time) order	*Imagine that you made an amazing discovery. Write about it.* *Write a story about finding an old treasure map.*
essay letter	order of space (top to bottom, bottom to top, etc.) chronological (time) order	*Describe your idea of the perfect day.* *Describe your favorite animal.*

Always start by reading the question and figuring out what it wants you to do. Do you have to persuade, explain, or tell a story? Rephrase the question in your own words to make sure that you understand it. **If you have a choice of topic, choose the one you know the most about and would most enjoy writing.** Then consider your audience and guidelines.

ma

Organize Your Essay

Your **audience** is your readers. On a standardized test, your reader will be someone you have never met. Some essays are even scored by machine! Then you won't know what your readers expect. In these cases, assume that you are writing for a grown-up like your teacher.

Your **guidelines** include the time, length, and structure of the exam. You might have 20 minutes to an hour to write. The length may be anywhere from one paragraph of 150 words to a four-or-five paragraph essay of 500 words. **Make sure you understand your audience and guidelines *before* you write a single word.**

Don't just start writing! Instead, take a few moments to decide how to structure your essay. Write an introduction that makes your point. Give examples in the body. Then write a conclusion. Here are some examples:

One paragraph
Introduction, one example, conclusion

Three paragraph essay
Introduction, one example, conclusion

Four paragraph essay
Introduction, two examples (one in each paragraph), conclusion

Five paragraph essay
Introduction, three examples (one in each paragraph), conclusion

express yourself!

ke a plan

JOT DOWN A QUICK OUTLINE. Here's a sample:

PROMPT: WHAT MAKES SOMEONE A SUCCESS?
Write an essay of 350-500 words explaining how you define "success."

PLAN

1ST PARAGRAPH	***Introduction*** Topic sentence (a question, quote, or brief story, for example) List three main examples Lead into 2nd paragraph
2ND PARAGRAPH	***Example 1: Success is helping others.*** *Detail*: Being a Big Brother or Big Sister *Detail:* Doing chores for neighbors (shoveling snow, raking leaves, running errands)
3RD PARAGRAPH	***Example 2: Success is helping the planet.*** *Detail*: Organizing the school recycling drive in May *Detail*: Planting oak trees on Arbor Day
4TH PARAGRAPH	***Example 3: Success is having love and meaningful work.*** *Detail*: Having family like Mom and friends like Taneka and Luigi *Detail*: Having a job you like, such as babysitting or tutoring
5TH PARAGRAPH	***Conclusion*** Topic sentence Summarize three main examples Conclude (state your opinion, call for action, or summarize and restate)

Use Specific Details and Examples

I kept six honest serving men
They taught me all I knew
Their names are What and Where and When
And How and Why and Who
—**Rudyard Kipling**

When you tell *what, where, when, how, why,* and *who,* you are providing specific details. Details make your writing clear, vivid, and interesting. They help you prove your point, too. Details also entertain your reader so your writing is fun to read. **What can you conclude from this? Details help you earn a high score on your writing.**

The chart below shows the main kinds of details you can use in your writing.

TYPE OF DETAIL	DEFINITION	EXAMPLE
Examples	Specific information about the concept	*Poppies are a symbol of consolation in times of death. In England, Australia, and Canada, people wear red poppies to honor soldiers who have died in war.*
Facts	Statements that can be proven	*Most roses have thorns or prickles.*
Descriptions	Words or phrases that tell *how* something looks, smells, tastes, sounds, or feels	*The mangy, sour-smelling lion shocked the kids with his fierce roar.*
Definitions	Statements that explain what something means	*Integrity means being truthful and honest.*
Statistics	Numbers used to give additional information	*Of the 452 middle school students who took the writing test, 78% passed.*
Reasons	Explanations that tell *why* something happened	*Tornadoes form where cold, dry, polar air meets warm, moist, tropical air.*

Write Clearly, Directly, and Precisely

Express your ideas clearly. Below are some examples.

> **The first example sounds awkward because the ideas are not parallel. Parallel ideas are in the same grammatical form.**

NOT PARALLEL *Mailing* a letter early is better than *to run* the risk of it arriving late.
          VERBAL NOUN   **INFINITIVE**

PARALLEL *Mailing* a letter early is better than *running* the risk of it arriving late.
       VERBAL NOUN   **VERBAL NOUN**

-or- PARALLEL *To mail* a letter early is better than *to run* the risk of it arriving late.
           INFINITIVE   **INFINITIVE**

> **The following example has an unclear pronoun. Who are the "he" and "him" in the second part of the sentence?**

UNCLEAR Jacob hugged my brother Sean, even though *he* didn't like *him* very much.
                                                ?   ?

CLEAR Jacob hugged my brother Sean, even though *Jacob* didn't like *Sean* very much.
                                            NOUN   **NOUN**

> **The following example lacks details.**

VAGUE Friends make me happy when I am sad.

DETAILED My friend *Zuzene* cheered me up *on Friday* by *bringing me a yellow*
              SPECIFIC NAME   **SPECIFIC DATE**   **SPECIFIC ACTION**
balloon with a smiley face on it.
     DESCRIPTION OF BALLOON

> **Avoid using big words just to impress your reader. Instead, use the word that fits the context.**

STUFFY Jack and Jill *ascended* the *escarpment* to *procure* an *ewer* of water.

CLEAR Jack and Jill *went up* the *hill* to *get* a *pail* of water.

One of the main reasons that students do poorly on essay tests is because they don't answer the question. Also, some of the details don't have anything to do with the question. Lastly, the ideas don't make sense because they're not organized. Below is the beginning of an essay. Notice how it stays on topic and has a clear method of organization:

PROMPT:
SOMETIMES, OUR PLANS DON'T WORK OUT THE WAY WE EXPECT.
Write about some times when your plans got cancelled. Explain what you did instead. Your essay should be 250-350 words long.

Read this model essay. The topic sentence, examples, and details are underlined in the first two paragraphs. *As you read, underline the examples and details in the last two paragraphs.*

INTRODUCTION — Everyone knows the saying, "You can't always get what you want."

TOPIC SENTENCE — It's true! For that reason, people need to make reasonable plans but be flexible when events change. This can help you have fun rather than just sitting on the couch staring at the TV remote.

EXAMPLE 1 — Plans to spend time at a friend's house can go awry. Last week, for instance, my friend Brett invited me to come over on Saturday night.

DETAILS — We planned to eat sausage pizza and play his new video games. "We have last-minute plans, Brett," his parents said. "We

DETAILS — just got two free tickets to the community theatre's production of *The Sound of Music*. Jason can't stay over when we're not home." We changed our plans and all went mini-golfing with Jason and Malek.

Stay on Topic and Stay Organized

Holidays don't always go as planned, either. For more than ten years, my family has hosted a big Thanksgiving celebration. At least 25 friends and relatives come for the day. Dad cooks a huge turkey—at least 30 pounds. Mom makes sweet potatoes dotted with marshmallows, green beans, and almonds, and the gravy. Aunt Felice brings her famous cornbread stuffing. Uncle Louie makes hot dogs. Of course, hot dogs don't go with a Thanksgiving meal, but everyone likes hot dogs in my house. Our friends Bob and Debbie bring pumpkin pies and cherry pies. Grandma YiaYia makes Greek pastries. Last Thanksgiving, we had a freak snowstorm! All the roads were closed so no one could get to our house. My parents just laughed. "We'll have a pre-Thanksgiving today," they said, "and another one next week." We had a lot of fun having two Thanksgivings.

answer
the
question

Events don't always work out the way we expect. My plans to spend time at Brett's house didn't go as we planned. Thanksgiving last year sure didn't, either. But in both cases, it was more fun when the plans didn't work out!

Proofread!

Even if you're very short on time, always proofread. This will help you catch careless errors that can cost you valuable points.

Try it now. Proofread the following passage for errors in spelling, capitalization, punctuation, and grammar.

My Aunt Millie and my Mother Marie are more then sister's—their best freinds. They allways helping each other out, especially when it come to cleaning house. Since there both "collectors," every june they has a huge garage sale at Aunt Millies brite blue house. For a week, they lug out doll after doll, teacup after teacup, hoping that someone will find these items useful. The lawn was carpeted with broken lamps, dented pots, and chipped dishes, by the end of the weekend, it has all magically dissapeared!

CORRECTED PARAGRAPH

My aunt Millie and my mother Marie are more than sisters—they're best friends. They always help each other out, especially when it comes to cleaning house. Since they're both "collectors," every June they have a huge garage sale at Aunt Millie's bright blue house. For a week, they lug out doll after doll, teacup after teacup, hoping that someone will find these items useful. The lawn is carpeted with broken lamps, dented pots, and chipped dishes. By the end of the weekend, it has all magically disappeared!

Sample Prompts

1. Write a letter to convince your parents to give you an allowance. If you already get an allowance, convince them to raise it.

2. Should community service be a requirement for graduation from middle school?

3. Should homework be eliminated? Why or why not?

4. Explain why honesty is or is not important in a friendship.

5. Explain who you consider to be your role model and why.

6. Friends are important, but everyone has a different opinion of what makes someone a good friend. Explain, in your opinion, what makes a good friend.

7. Imagine that you have made a very important discovery that will make you famous. Write a story in which you tell about your discovery and how you made it.

8. What is your perfect day? Write a story about it.

9. Write a story about having a super power. How would you use this power?

10. Describe what you think the world will be like 100 years from now.

11. Describe a special event you attended, such as a fair or sporting event.

12. Describe your school at lunchtime.

get creative

notes

CHAPTER 7: **Write Great Essays for Standardized Tests**

CHAPTER

8

Do you panic when you have to take a multiple-choice test? Do you believe you're better off taking an essay test because at least you can explain yourself? If so, you're not alone! But objective-question standardized tests don't have to cause panic. As with all tests, you can do better on objective-question standardized tests if you know how to take them. That's what this chapter will teach you.

Learn
How to Take
Standardized Tests
with Objective Questions

Practice Multiple-Choice Items

Circle the correct answer to each question. As you take the test, think about the process you use to answer the questions. What clues in each statement do you use?

1. **Which adaptation best enables polar bears to live in cold climates?**
   - Ⓐ ability to sleep during the winter
   - Ⓑ talent for finding food in many places
   - Ⓒ fierce claws and large size
   - Ⓓ thick fat and heavy fur

2. **Which flightless birds live only in the South Pole?**
   - Ⓐ penguins
   - Ⓑ geese
   - Ⓒ owls
   - Ⓓ seagulls

3. **Scientists divide the world into different climate zones because**
   - Ⓐ people like to live in different climates so they have a variety of weather.
   - Ⓑ climate refers to the average weather conditions in a region over a long period of time.
   - Ⓒ climate varies all over the world due to location and geography.
   - Ⓓ climate has little or no effect on your life when you are young.

4. **Climate is affected by all the following factors but**
   - Ⓐ winds
   - Ⓑ the equator
   - Ⓒ sunlight
   - Ⓓ oceans

5. **The closer to the poles you go, the less sunlight there is. How does this fact affect the climate of the North and South Poles?**
   - Ⓐ These regions get more sunlight.
   - Ⓑ It is colder there.
   - Ⓒ More people live there.
   - Ⓓ The climate changes rapidly.

6. **Antarctica is**
   - Ⓐ also called the South Pole.
   - Ⓑ a research lab and home to Eskimos.
   - Ⓒ covered by ice in winter only.
   - Ⓓ all of the above

7. **A temperate climate zone has**
   - Ⓐ hot, humid weather and high rainfall.
   - Ⓑ cold summers and warm winters.
   - Ⓒ warm summers and cold winters.
   - Ⓓ very cold winters with lots of snow.

8. **Climate is relatively stable over decades because**
   - Ⓐ weather patterns change little, especially over mountains and deserts.
   - Ⓑ trade winds blow north from the subtropics to the equator.
   - Ⓒ weather forecasts are rarely unreliable so you never know what clothes to wear.
   - Ⓓ climate is influenced by things that change slowly, like oceans and mountains.

ANSWERS: **1.** D, **2.** A, **3.** C, **4.** B, **5.** B, **6.** A, **7.** C, **8.** D

Ace Multiple-Choice Items

Multiple-choice items are the most common format you'll find on standardized tests. This means you will have many multiple-choice tests during school—and after! As a result, it's important to learn how to take these tests successfully. The following hints can help you do your best.

1. *Read every answer choice.*

Read every choice before you mark your answer. Even if you're sure that choice (a) is correct, read all the way to the last choice. You may find that another answer is even better than your original choice. This is the case with item #1. Look for an adaptation that *best* affects a bear's ability to survive fierce winters. The ability to sleep during the winter helps, but the bear's thick fat and heavy fur are even more important. In fact, it is the most important adaptation.

2. *Look for clues in the sentence.*

Often the sentence contains clues that help you figure out the answer. Look back at item #2. The clue word is "flightless." All the other birds listed can fly. Only penguins cannot fly.

3. *Use process of elimination.*

Start by crossing off any choices that are silly. These are called "distractors." Look back at item #3. Choices (a) and (d) are silly. Then look more deeply. Choice (b) makes sense, but it doesn't answer the question. That leaves you with the correct choice, (c).

4. *Look for key words.*

Multiple-choice questions that contain the words **not**, **but**, and **except** are asking you to find the opposite. These questions are tricky because they are easy to misread. Look back at item #4. Three choices are true. One choice is not. You are asked to find the choice that is not true. Every factor but the equator affects climate. Thus, the correct choice is (b).

5. *Predict the answer.*

As you read the question, think about what the answer should be. Then try to find that answer. Use this method on item #5. You know that there is less sunlight in the winter. Winters are cold. Therefore, you can predict that less sunlight would make the North and South poles colder.

6. *Watch the all of the above choice.*

For the answer to be *all of the above*, every part of every choice has to be correct. Look back at item #6. Choices (b) and (c) are not completely true. Antarctica is a research lab, but Eskimos live in the Arctic. Antarctica is covered by ice all the time. Only choice (a) is completely true, so (d) cannot be true.

7. *Look for choices that are opposites.*

If two choices are opposites, chances are one of them is correct. Look back at item 7. Choices (b) and (c) are opposites. Choice (c) is correct.

8. *Use grammar clues.*

All multiple-choice questions follow the rules of grammar. First choose the answer that makes the most sense to you. Then plug the answer into the rest of the question to see if it is grammatically correct. Look at item 8. Eliminate choices (a) and (b) because they don't fit with the stem. Read them aloud and you will hear that they sound awkward.

HERE ARE SOME MORE HINTS:

9. *Get a plan.*

There are several ways to tackle multiple choice questions. Many people use this method: Work from start to finish, answering each question. If you can't answer a question, put a mark next to it. If you have time, go back and answer these questions. Here's another method: Answer the easiest questions first. Then go back and answer the harder questions. Choose the plan that works best for you. Having a plan helps you work steadily. It also helps you avoid panic.

10. *Work steadily.*

Don't spend too much time on any one question. Try to answer as many questions as you can. This increases your chance of earning a good grade on the test.

11. *Check your work and be neat!*

Make sure that you bubbled in every answer correctly. If you skipped some questions, be extra careful. Make sure that you erased all stray marks. Double-check that you have marked your answers firmly enough that they can be read.

12. *Guess!*

If there is a penalty for wrong answers, guess only if you can eliminate some answers. For every answer you eliminate, you increase your odds of guessing correctly.

Practice True-False Items

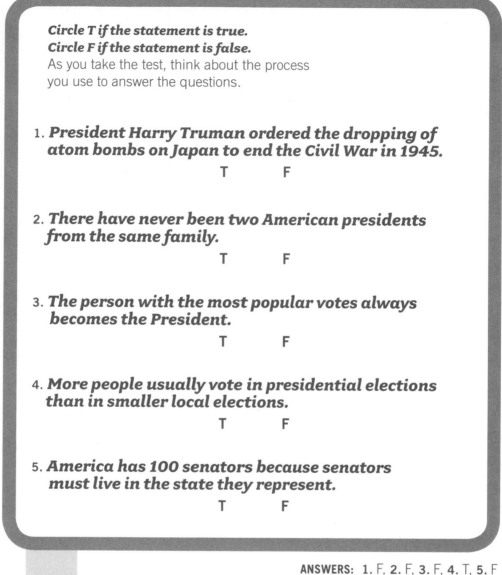

Circle T if the statement is true.
Circle F if the statement is false.
As you take the test, think about the process
you use to answer the questions.

1. **President Harry Truman ordered the dropping of atom bombs on Japan to end the Civil War in 1945.**

   T   F

2. **There have never been two American presidents from the same family.**

   T   F

3. **The person with the most popular votes always becomes the President.**

   T   F

4. **More people usually vote in presidential elections than in smaller local elections.**

   T   F

5. **America has 100 senators because senators must live in the state they represent.**

   T   F

ANSWERS: 1. F, 2. F, 3. F, 4. T, 5. F

plan

Triumph Over True/False Tests

True/false questions require you to recognize a fact or idea. They also check your reading comprehension. As a result, you have to memorize information. You also have to read very carefully. Try the following hints.

1. *The entire sentence must be true.*
If any one part of the sentence is false, the whole sentence is false. Even if part of it is true, any false information makes it false.

Look back at item #1. The first half is true: President Harry Truman did order the dropping of atom bombs on Japan in 1945. But the second half is false. It was not the Civil War. It was World War II. Since part of the statement is false, the entire statement is false.

2. *Beware of negative words.* Negative words include **no**, **not**, **cannot**, **never**, **not at all**, **no one**, **absolutely not**. Statements with a negative word are rarely true. Look at item 2. There have been two presidents from the same family. The Adams and the Bush families are examples.

3. *Beware of absolute words.*
Absolute words include **always**, **every**, **entirely**, **all**, **all the time**, **everyone**. Statements are rarely true with one of these absolute words. John Quincy Adams and George W. Bush, for example, did not have a popular majority.

4. *Look for words that show shades of meaning.* Words like **sometimes**, **often**, **frequently**, **many**, **most**, **rarely**, **sometimes**, **occasionally**, **generally**, **ordinarily** often indicate true statements. That's because they show that the statement is not completely right or wrong.

focus on fact

5. *Check that the statement is logical.*
Two statements can be true but if they are linked by a word that makes them false, they are false. Look back at item 5. It is true that America has 100 senators. It is true that senators must live in the state they represent. But item 5 is false. We have 100 senators because each state has two senators.

6. *Guess!* Should you guess on true/false questions? Yes! That's because you have a fifty percent chance of getting the answer right.

Conquer Short-Answer Tests

Short-answer tests may ask you to write one word (fill-in-the-blank questions), a group of words, a sentence, or even a paragraph. Follow these suggestions to do well on these tests.

1. *Study facts.*
Short-answer tests are recall tests. You have to remember facts. To prepare, concentrate on vocabulary and key details.

2. *Be sure you answer the question.*
Answer what you are asked.

3. *Write clearly and briefly.*
Focus on giving the important points in a clear and concise manner. Don't be too wordy.

4. *Look for links in ideas.*
As you read the sentence, substitute the word *blank* for the blank. This helps you figure out what's missing and how the sentence will sound when complete.

5. *Use common sense to make sure your answer is logical.*
If your answer doesn't match what you already know, revise it. An answer can be true and still be wrong. The correct choice is the one that best answers the question, not necessarily the one that is true.

Sample Short-Answer Test

DIRECTIONS: *Answer all questions from this part.* Each correct answer will receive 5 points. *Write your answers in the lines provided.* You have 15 minutes to complete this part of the test.

Gentlemen of the Jury: The best friend a man has in the world may turn against him and become his enemy. His son or daughter that he has reared with loving care may prove ungrateful. Those who are nearest and dearest to us, those whom we trust with our happiness and our good name may become traitors to their faith. The money that a man has, he may lose. It flies away from him, perhaps when he needs it most. A man's reputation may be sacrificed in a moment of ill-considered action. The people who are prone to fall on their knees to do us honor when success is with us, may be the first to throw the stone of malice when failure settles its cloud upon our heads.

The one absolutely unselfish friend that man can have in this selfish world, the one that never deserts him, the one that never proves ungrateful or treacherous is his dog. A man's dog stands by him in prosperity and in poverty, in health and in sickness. He will sleep on the cold ground, where the wintry winds blow and the snow drives fiercely, if only he may be near his master's side. He will kiss the hand that has no food to offer. He will lick the wounds and sores that come in encounters with the roughness of the world. He guards the sleep of his pauper master as if he were a prince. When all other friends desert, he remains. When riches take wings, and reputation falls to pieces, he is as constant in his love as the sun in its journey through the heavens.

If fortune drives the master forth, an outcast in the world, friendless and homeless, the faithful dog asks no higher privilege than that of accompanying him, to guard him against danger, to fight against his enemies. And when the last scene of all comes, and death takes his master in its embrace and his body is laid away in the cold ground, no matter if all other friends pursue their way, there by the graveside will the noble dog be found, his head between his paws, his eyes sad, but open in alert watchfulness, faithful and true even in death.

1. **What does the speaker say about friends?**

_____

_____

2. **Summarize the speaker's opinion of relatives?**

_____

_____

3. **Explain the speaker's view of money.**

_____

_____

4. **Summarize the speaker's opinion of dogs.**

_____

_____

5. **The speaker delivered this speech while representing a man who sued another man for killing his dog. This is his summation to the jury. Do you think he won his case? Why or why not?**

_____

_____

ANSWERS: **1.** They are not trustworthy; they may turn against you. **2.** They may be ungrateful. **3.** People can lose their money, so money is fleeting. **4.** They are your only true friends. **5.** The man did win his case because his argument is specific, emotional, and persuasive.

notes

You've learned that standardized tests take many different forms. For example, some tests ask you to solve equations. Other tests can include multiple-choice, short-answer, and/or essay questions. Still others are DBQs. These tests have a special format.

Do Your

Best

on Document-Based Questions (DBQs)

DBQs are writing tests. You will have to write some short answers and an essay. DBQs are also different in another big way: they include both visual prompts and text. DBQs are often on standardized social studies and English assessments. The College Board, for instance, gives standardized history tests in the DBQ format; many states include DBQs on their yearly assessments.

What are DBQs?

DBQs are Document-Based Questions.
These tests ask you to write about historical records. Historical records include many different kinds of documents. Some documents are famous such as the *Declaration of Independence*, the *Gettysburg Address*, and the *Emancipation Proclamation*. Others are not well known. Below are some historical records that are often used on DBQ tests:

architectural drawings
blueprints
birth certificates
crime statistics
databases of marriages
drawings and cartoons
e-mail
films
last wills and testaments
letters
maps
photographs
political cartoons
political writings
postcards
posters
proclamations
ships' logs
speeches
tax assessment records
timelines

Historical records could be hundreds of years old, or they could have been created yesterday. But no matter when they were made, all historical records contain useful information about people, places, events, and subjects.

evaluate
analyze

DBQs ask you to think critically. This means you don't just recall facts.
Instead, you interpret, clarify, analyze, and evaluate information.
You look for point of view and bias. (Bias is the slant or opinion in a document.)
You might have to tell the difference between fact (truth) and fiction (make-believe),
too. **DBQs test your ability to draw conclusions.** The process looks like this:

What I know + What I See on the Document = Conclusions

interpret
clarify

A typical DBQ is a group of several original sources. The test may have two sources or as many as eight. Each source will be labeled by a letter, starting with "Document A." Some sources will be quotes or passages. Others will be political cartoons, maps, posters, or other visuals. In most cases, the sources provide different views on the same event that you will have to analyze.

Here is a sample DBQ.

The following question is based on the accompanying documents 1-5. The question tests your ability to analyze and interpret the documents. Then you will write an essay which uses information from the documents. Study the rubric at the end of the question. It shows how your essay will be graded.

DIRECTIONS: *For Part A, read each document and answer the questions that follow. For Part B, write an essay. Use the information you gathered in Part A and your outside knowledge as you write the essay.*

"I Will Fight No More Forever"
SPEECH BY CHIEF JOSEPH OF THE NEZ PERCE, OCTOBER 5, 1877

I am tired of fighting. Our chiefs are killed. Looking Glass is dead. Toohulhulsote is dead. The old men are all dead. It is the young men who say yes or no. He who led the young men is dead.

It is cold and we have no blankets. The little children are freezing to death. My people, some of them, have run away to the hills and have no blankets, no food. No one knows where they are—perhaps freezing to death. I want to have time to look for my children and see how many I can find. Maybe I shall find them among the dead. Hear me, my chiefs. I am tired. My heart is sick and sad. From where the sun now stands, I will fight no more forever.

1. *Why doesn't Chief Joseph want to fight anymore?*

2. *What is the tone or feeling of this speech?*

3. *Why do you think Chief Joseph gave this speech? What was his purpose?*

This political cartoon shows a woman and child being squeezed by a snake. The woman and child stand for pioneers. The snake stands for Native Americans. The sign reads "Uncle Sam's Pet: Hands Off!" Uncle Sam is feeding the Native Americans while the pioneers' home burns. This cartoon protested the government's policy of helping Native Americans in the winter after the Native Americans had attacked settlers in the summer.

1. *How are the Native Americans shown in this cartoon?*

....

....

2. *The US government helped the Native Americans through the winter after the Native Americans had attacked settlers through the summer. How does the cartoonist feel about this government policy?*

....

....

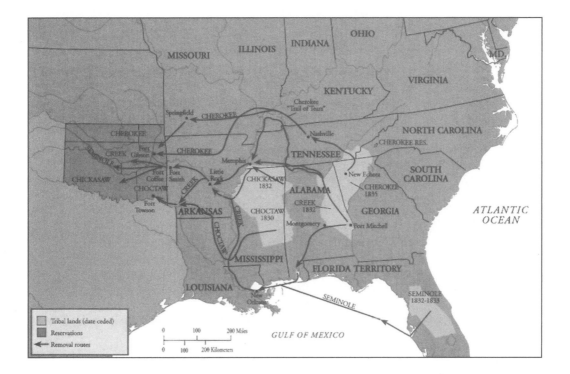

1. *This map shows the "Trail of Tears." This was the forced removal of the Cherokee in the winter of 1838–39. Calculate the distance the Cherokee traveled from Georgia to their new home in Oklahoma.*

2. *Explain why the "Trail of Tears" got its name.*

This photograph from the mid-1870s shows
a pile of bison skulls waiting to be ground for fertilizer.

1. *Why would settlers and the government destroy
   the vast herds of bison?*

....

....

2. *How do you think the Native Americans felt about
   the destruction of the bison, one of their main foods?*

....

....

DOCUMENT E

Near the end of King Philip's War, a group of Nipmunk and Narragansett Indians attacked Lancaster. They burned the town and captured many of the settlers. Mary Rowlandson and her three children were among them. The following is an excerpt from Rowlandson's diary.

On the tenth of February 1675, came the Indians with great numbers upon Lancaster: their first coming was about sunrising; hearing the noise of some guns, we looked out; several houses were burning, and the smoke ascending to heaven. There were five persons taken in one house; the father, and the mother and a child, they knocked on the head; the other two they took and carried away alive. There were two others, who being out of their garrison upon some occasion were set upon; one was knocked on the head, the other escaped; another there was who running along was shot and wounded, and fell down...the Indians getting up upon the roof of the barn, had advantage to shoot down upon them over their fortification. Thus these murderous wretches went on, burning, and destroying before them.

1. *Why did the Native Americans attack Lancaster?*

....

....

2. *What words show Mary Rowlandson's feeling about these Native Americans?*

....

....

Part B

HISTORICAL CONTEXT

Native Americans and newcomers did not always get along well. American settlers and pioneers held differing viewpoints on Native Americans. So did government officials and business people.

TASK

Using at least three of the documents and your knowledge of American history, write an essay in which you

* *describe different attitudes people in the 19th century had toward Native Americans.*
* *provide reasons for their attitudes.*

A rubric appears on many DBQ tests. The rubric shows you what the scorers are looking for as they grade your essay. Read the rubric carefully. Here is a sample:

RUBRIC:

SCORE	RANKING	REASONS
3	Excellent	*Answers the question thoughtfully and intelligently; provides specific detail; shows understanding of the documents by using them to support the argument; addresses the opinions or biases in the documents; includes outside information; presents information in a logical and well-organized essay*
2	Good	*Answers the question; provides some detail from the articles; has a method of organization; does not address all the biases in the articles; includes little outside information; may contain small misunderstandings*
1	Poor	*Provides some answers but missing key details; may address only part of the question; contains little detail; has no outside information or mistaken information; does not have a clear method of organization*
0	No credit	*Does not answer the question; misinterprets the question or documents; jumbles ideas; includes inappropriate information*

How to Answer a DBQ Test

Use this method to answer document-based question tests.

STEP #1

Study each document, one at a time. Look carefully at the visuals. Read the text several times to make sure you understand it. In your own words, summarize what each document shows. This helps you make sure that you understand the documents. Then answer each question. Stick to the facts. Write in complete sentences.

STEP #2

Read the grading rubric. Rephrase the task in your own words. Pay special attention to the following key words in the essay question:

DESCRIBE: Tell about something using words that appeal to the five senses.
DISCUSS: Make observations about something using facts, reasoning, and argument.
SHOW: State a position or idea and give facts to support it.
EXPLAIN: Provide specific reasons for something.

Then choose the documents that you understood best. Be sure to choose the correct number of documents you need, as listed in the assignment. If no number is listed, use half and one more. For instance, if there are six documents, use four. (Half of six is three. Three + one = four.)

STEP #4

Write the essay. Look back at the documents as you write. This will help you draw specific details from them. If you are working with a text, quote important passages. If you are working with a visual such as a cartoon, describe parts of it that answer the question.

STEP #3

Make an outline.
Organize your essay in three parts: an introduction, body, and conclusion. Below is a sample format. Each Roman numeral stands for a paragraph.

I. INTRODUCTION: Restate the question in your own words. State your main idea. List the documents you will use.

II. DOCUMENT #1: Use specific elements from the document and what you already know to answer the question.

III. DOCUMENT #2: Use specific elements from the document and what you already know to answer the question.

IV. DOCUMENT #3: Use specific elements from the document and what you already know to answer the question.

V. CONCLUSION: Summarize your main idea.

STEP #5

Edit and proofread the essay. Make sure that you have really answered the question. Check that you have included specific details, examples, and facts.

Top Ten Hints for Earning a High Score on a DBQ

1. *Check the date of each document.* Make sure you understand the historical period when they were produced.

2. *Analyze the tone of each document.* For example, the tone of Chief Joseph's speech is sad. This helps you understand his feelings and purpose. From the tone, you know that Chief Joseph is surrendering.

3. *Remember that the documents are not necessarily facts.* Often, they just express the opinion of the writer or artist. This is shown in Document B, for instance. Some people may agree with the cartoonist's anger toward Native Americans. Many other people may feel compassion, in contrast.

4. *Don't force your views on the document by making it mean something that it doesn't mean.* For instance, Document D shows that settlers and the government killed all the bison to drive the Native Americans from the land. If they did not have food, the Native Americans would be forced to leave. The settlers did not kill the bison to make Native Americans into vegetarians, for instance.

5. *The scorer knows the documents well so don't summarize them.* Instead, make specific references to the document that directly answers the question. For instance, say, "Grant Hamilton, the cartoonist who drew 'The Nation's Ward,' resented the Native Americans. This is clear from the picture. First, he shows the Native Americans as a savage snake. The snake is squeezing a young pioneer family. Uncle Sam is feeding the Native Americans while the pioneers' home burns. The cartoon protests the U.S. policy of helping Native Americans through the winter after the Native Americans had attacked settlers through the summer."

6. *The documents are often given in chronological order, but you do not have to use them that way.* Use them in the order that make the most sense to you.

7. *You don't have to use all the documents.* You are usually better off not trying to use them all, because that is too much information.

8. *Answer the question you are asked.* Address each part of the question.

9. *Remember that there is no one right answer on the DBQ.* Your answer will be graded on how well you supported your view with details, facts, and examples.

10. *Always save time to proofread your answers.* This can help you catch careless errors.

Self Test

Complete the DBQ in this chapter. Use your own paper.

CHAPTER 10

You've learned so much about standardized tests! One of the most important things you've learned is that "practice makes perfect." Below are some practice tests. Take these tests under test conditions: in a quiet room, in one sitting. After you score your answers, review the test. Return to the chapters that cover the material you missed.

Sample
Standardized
Practice Tests
Tests

Test #1 20 QUESTIONS 40 MINUTES

DIRECTIONS: Each sentence below is missing one or two words. Under each sentence are possible answers. Choose the answer that *best* completes each sentence. Fill in the circle of your answer.

1. *The play's reviews had been excellent and the theatre was filled to capacity, but we found the show _____.*
   - Ⓐ surprising
   - Ⓑ remarkable
   - Ⓒ innovative
   - Ⓓ exciting
   - Ⓔ dreary

2. *When the toddler missed his nap, he became agitated and _____.*
   - Ⓐ distressed
   - Ⓑ serene
   - Ⓒ cheerful
   - Ⓓ calm
   - Ⓔ ambitious

3. *The cook enjoyed baking elaborate desserts, but found everyday tasks like peeling potatoes and steaming vegetables _____.*
   - Ⓐ exhilarating
   - Ⓑ tedious
   - Ⓒ enjoyable
   - Ⓓ standard
   - Ⓔ normal

4. *Although her fingerprints were never found on the evidence, her involvement was obvious: she had _____ and _____ the theft by selling the stolen jewelry.*
   - Ⓐ delayed…prompted
   - Ⓑ assisted…stopped
   - Ⓒ shunned…obstructed
   - Ⓓ helped…abetted
   - Ⓔ hampered…supported

5. *The dance team in the contest was* _____ *so they were* _____ *with flowers from their ecstatic fans.*
- Ⓐ triumphant…challenged
- Ⓑ successful…confronted
- Ⓒ victorious…rewarded
- Ⓓ doomed… opposed
- Ⓔ ineffective…regaled

DIRECTIONS: Questions 6 and 7 are based on the following passage. Fill in the circle of your answer.

Huge Storms Converge

1 The two biggest storms in the solar system are about to bump into each other in plain view of backyard telescopes. Storm #1 is the Great Red Spot, twice as wide as Earth itself, with winds blowing 350 mph. The behemoth has been spinning around Jupiter for hundreds of years. Storm #2 is Oval BA, also known as "Red Jr.," a youngster of a

5 storm only six years old. Compared to the Great Red Spot, Red Jr. is half-sized, able to swallow Earth merely once, but it blows just as hard as its older cousin. The two are converging. Closest approach: the 4th of July, according to Amy Simon-Miller of the Goddard Space Flight Center who has been monitoring the storms using the Hubble

10 Space Telescope. "There won't be a head-on collision," she says. "The Great Red Spot is not going to 'eat' Oval BA or anything like that." But the storms' outer bands will pass quite close to one another—and no one knows exactly what will happen. Amateur astronomers are already monitoring the event.

Source: NASA

6. *As used in this passage, behemoth most nearly means*
- Ⓐ storm.
- Ⓑ monster.
- Ⓒ top.
- Ⓓ mystery.
- Ⓔ oldster.

7. *Which conclusion is best supported by this paragraph?*

Ⓐ The author, an astronomer, is very afraid of the damage these storms will cause on Earth because their winds are so fierce.

Ⓑ Storms such as these occur all the time in space, but are still cause for serious alarm.

Ⓒ Professional and amateur astronomers are closely monitoring these fascinating storms, although they pose no danger to Earth.

Ⓓ If the storms hit each other, their power will dissipate and they will float away harmlessly.

Ⓔ Storms in space can be used to predict storms on earth with remarkable accuracy, according to professional astronomers.

DIRECTIONS: Questions 8-11 are based on the following passage. Fill in the circle of your answer.

Dolley Payne Todd Madison

1   Blessed with a desire to please and a willingness to be pleased, Dolley made her home the center of society when James Madison began, in 1801, his eight years as Jefferson's Secretary of State. She assisted at the White House when the President asked her help in receiving ladies, and presided at the first inaugural ball in Washington when her

5   husband became Chief Executive in 1809.

Dolley's social graces made her famous. Her political acumen, prized by her husband, is less renowned, though her gracious tact smoothed many a quarrel. Hostile statesmen, difficult envoys from Spain or Tunisia, warrior chiefs from the west,

10 flustered youngsters—she always welcomed everyone. Forced to flee from the White House by a British army during the War of 1812, she returned to find the mansion in ruins. Undaunted by temporary quarters, she entertained as skillfully as ever.

Source: www.whitehouse.gov

8. *The tone or feeling of this passage is best described as*

Ⓐ critical.

Ⓑ scary.

Ⓒ sympathetic.

Ⓓ neutral.

Ⓔ admiring.

9. _As used in this passage, acumen most nearly means_
Ⓐ interest.
Ⓑ unawareness.
Ⓒ charm.
Ⓓ ignorance.
Ⓔ wisdom.

10. _Dolley Madison is best described as_
Ⓐ a skilled and gracious hostess and politician.
Ⓑ an accomplished writer, editor, and reporter.
Ⓒ a lucky person in the right place at the right time.
Ⓓ a coward who ran from the first sign of trouble.
Ⓔ someone easily shaken by unexpected events.

11. _An envoy is most likely a(n)_
Ⓐ oddball.
Ⓑ teenager.
Ⓒ spy.
Ⓓ diplomat.
Ⓔ soldier.

DIRECTIONS: In this section, solve each problem. You can use any space on the test as scratch paper. Then choose the best answer. Fill in the circle of your answer.

12. _If A = 4x - 2, and A = 14, then x =_
Ⓐ 6
Ⓑ 2
Ⓒ 2.75
Ⓓ 4
Ⓔ 14

13. _In a deck of 52 cards, 13 of them are hearts._
   What percentage of the cards are NOT hearts?
Ⓐ 4%
Ⓑ 13%
Ⓒ 25%
Ⓓ 39%
Ⓔ 75%

14. **If the probability of picking a blue sock from your drawer is 0.3, then if you randomly picked 20 socks out of the drawer, about how many would be blue?**
   Ⓐ 0
   Ⓑ 1
   Ⓒ 3
   Ⓓ 6
   Ⓔ 20

15. **Which answer is closest to 7,981 x 10,013?**
   Ⓐ 8,000,000
   Ⓑ 9,000,000
   Ⓒ 80,000,000
   Ⓓ 90,000,000
   Ⓔ 800,000,000

16. **Which number falls between $\frac{1}{2}$ and $\frac{1}{3}$?**
   Ⓐ 66%
   Ⓑ 0.1116
   Ⓒ 0.444

   Ⓓ $\frac{10}{14}$

   Ⓔ $\frac{2}{3}$

DIRECTIONS: The following questions require you to identify errors in grammar, usage, style, and mechanics. Not every sentence has an error, and no sentence will have more than one error. If there is an error, choose the underlined part that must be changed to make the sentence correct. Fill in the correct circle on your answer sheet. If the sentence does not have an error, fill in circle E.

17. _**Twins**_ have fascinated people for _**centuries**_, _**according**_ to legend,
    A   B

the twin founders of Rome, _**Romulus and Remus**_, _**were raised**_ by
                          C   D

a wolf. _**No error.**_
     E

Ⓐ   Ⓑ   Ⓒ   Ⓓ   Ⓔ

18. _**Its'**_ true that people _**shouldn't**_ hold _**grudges, but**_ many people like
    A   B   C

my _**Aunt Edna**_ do anyway. _**No error.**_
     D   E

Ⓐ   Ⓑ   Ⓒ   Ⓓ   Ⓔ

19. Marc _**didn't have no**_ _**money, so**_ he decided to get an after-school
            A   B

job _**cleaning tables**_ and _**washing dishes**_ at the diner. _**No error.**_
      C   D   E

Ⓐ   Ⓑ   Ⓒ   Ⓓ   Ⓔ

20. _**Nico is a better soccer**_ player than _**Hubert, but**_ Ralph is the
           A   B

**best soccer player of all** because _**he practices every day**_ and on
       C   D

weekends. _**No error.**_
        E

Ⓐ   Ⓑ   Ⓒ   Ⓓ   Ⓔ

Test #2 20 QUESTIONS 40 MINUTES

DIRECTIONS: In this section, solve each problem. You can use any space on the test as scratch paper. Then choose the best answer. Fill in the circle of your answer.

1. *Which of the follow is not equivalent?*
   Ⓐ $\sqrt{36}$
   Ⓑ $6\sqrt{10}$
   Ⓒ $2\sqrt{9}$
   Ⓓ $3\sqrt{4}$
   Ⓔ 6

2. *If the probability of picking a chocolate-chip cookie from a bag of mixed cookies is 0.25, then if you randomly picked 40 cookies out of the bag, about how many would be chocolate-chip?*
   Ⓐ 1
   Ⓑ 4
   Ⓒ 10
   Ⓓ 25
   Ⓔ 40

3. *Five servers receive the following tips. Whose was the greatest?*
   Ⓐ 20% of $100
   Ⓑ 15% of $200
   Ⓒ 10% of $250
   Ⓓ 20% of $175
   Ⓔ 15% of $150

4. *If the hour hand of a clock is at exactly a 135° angle with 12, what time must it be?*
   Ⓐ 9:00
   Ⓑ 9:15
   Ⓒ 6:00
   Ⓓ 12:45
   Ⓔ 9:45

5. **To convert millimeters to meters, you should:**
Ⓐ multiply by 10
Ⓑ divide by 100
Ⓒ multiply by 100
Ⓓ multiply by 1000
Ⓔ divide by 1000

6. **If $x \div 5 = y$, what is $x \div 10$?**
Ⓐ y
Ⓑ y ÷ 2
Ⓒ y ÷ 3
Ⓓ 2y
Ⓔ 6y

7. **John walks at an average speed of 3.2 miles per hour. How long does it take him to go 4 miles?**
Ⓐ 4.8 minutes
Ⓑ 48 minutes
Ⓒ 53 minutes
Ⓓ 75 minutes
Ⓔ 90 minutes

8. **If you roll two six-sided dice, what is the probability that the combined total shown will be greater than 9?**

Ⓐ $\dfrac{10}{14}$　　Ⓑ $\dfrac{7}{36}$　　Ⓒ $\dfrac{1}{12}$　　Ⓓ $\dfrac{3}{36}$　　Ⓔ 0

9. **I have a wall that is 10 feet high and 18 feet long. There is a window set into the wall that is 5 feet high and 4 feet wide. If I need to paint the wall, and 1 quart of paint covers 20 square feet, how much paint do I need?**
Ⓐ 0.8 quarts of paint
Ⓓ 8 quarts of paint
Ⓒ 8.8 quarts of paint
Ⓓ 9.6 quarts of paint
Ⓔ 20 quarts of paint

10. **"Some perfect squares are less than 100."** Which of the following statements is true according to the statement above?
Ⓐ 100 is a perfect square.
Ⓑ All perfect squares are less than 100.
Ⓒ All numbers less than 100 are perfect squares.
Ⓓ Some perfect squares are greater than 100.
Ⓔ No perfect squares are greater than 100.

DIRECTIONS: Each sentence below is missing one or two words.
Under each sentence are possible answers.
Choose the answer that best completes each sentence. Fill in the circle of your answer.

11. <u>In her</u> <u>leisure time</u> after <u>school,</u> Maria enjoys hiking, swimming,
   A   B   C

  and <u>to ride a bicycle.</u> <u>No error.</u>
           D   E

Ⓐ   Ⓑ   Ⓒ   Ⓓ   Ⓔ

12. <u>During the flood, the</u> water rose <u>fifteen inches</u> but then <u>recceeded</u>
     A   B   C   D

  to its normal level. <u>No error.</u>
                 E

Ⓐ   Ⓑ   Ⓒ   Ⓓ   Ⓔ

13. <u>Vicks</u> book was <u>more interesting</u> reading than he <u>expected, so</u> he
   A   B   C

  spent most of <u>Thanksgiving</u> reading! <u>No error.</u>
                   D   E

Ⓐ   Ⓑ   Ⓒ   Ⓓ   Ⓔ

14. <u>My brother Chris</u> ordered <u>French dressing</u> on his <u>salad but</u> Shawn
         A   B   C

  preferred <u>Russian dressing</u> on his salad. <u>No error.</u>
               D   E

Ⓐ   Ⓑ   Ⓒ   Ⓓ   Ⓔ

15. <u>*Our new* puppy *Spot's toy's*</u> <u>included an old</u> <u>shoe, a</u> <u>stuffed bear,</u>
       A   B   C
<u>*and a chewed-up blanket.*</u> <u>*No error.*</u>
            D   E

Ⓐ   Ⓑ   Ⓒ   Ⓓ   Ⓔ

DIRECTIONS: Questions 16-20 are based on the following passage.
Fill in the circle of your answer.

Algebra

1   The word "algebra" comes from the Arabic word "al-jabr" from the title of the
book written in 820. The origins of algebra can be traced to the ancient Babylonians,
who developed an advanced arithmetical system with which they were able to do
calculations in an algebraic fashion. With this system, they were able to apply formula

5   and calculate solutions for unknown values for a class of problems solved today by
using linear equations, quadratic equations, and indeterminate linear equations.
By contrast, most Egyptians, Indian, Greek and Chinese mathematicians in the first
millennium BC usually solved such equations by geometric methods.

10   Indian mathematicians wrote treatises on algebraic means of solving equations
from the end of the first millennium BC, followed by Hellenistic mathematicians from
the early first millennium AD. Al-Khwarizmi is often considered the "father of algebra"
(though that title is also given to Diophantus), as much of his works on reduction are
still in use today. Another Persian mathematician Omar Khayyam developed algebraic

15   geometry and found the general geometric solution of the cubic equation. The Indian
mathematicians Mahavira and Bhaskara, and the Chinese mathematician Zhu Shijie,
solved various cubic, quartic, quintic and higher-order polynomial equations.

16. *Algebra was started by mathematicians from ancient*
Ⓐ Babylonia.
Ⓑ India.
Ⓒ Greece.
Ⓓ China.
Ⓔ Persia.

17. *All of the following cultures contributed to the creation of Algebra except*
Ⓐ Persian.
Ⓑ Indian.
Ⓒ American.
Ⓓ Greek.
Ⓔ Chinese.

18. *Treatises are most likely*
Ⓐ web pages.
Ⓑ essays.
Ⓒ speeches.
Ⓓ arguments.
Ⓔ letters.

19. *It can be inferred from this passage that*
Ⓐ Algebra has not changed much from ancient days.
Ⓑ there are different ways to solve equations.
Ⓒ all math, but especially Algebra, is very complex.
Ⓓ no one is really sure how Algebra was created.
Ⓔ people created Algebra because they had a need for it.

20. *This document is most likely a(n)*
Ⓐ graduation speech.
Ⓑ fable.
Ⓒ magazine piece.
Ⓓ newspaper article.
Ⓔ encyclopedia entry.

Test #3 20 QUESTIONS 40 MINUTES

DIRECTIONS: The two passages below are followed by questions about their content and the relationship between the passages. Fill in the circle of your answer.

Passage 1

1   Napoleon built a 500,000 strong Grand Army which used modern tactics and improvisation in battle to sweep across Europe and acquire an empire for France. But in 1812, the seemingly invincible Napoleon made the fateful decision to invade Russia. He advanced deep into that vast country, eventually reaching Moscow in September. He

5   found Moscow had been burned by the Russians and could not support the hungry French Army over the long winter. Thus Napoleon was forced to begin a long retreat, and saw his army decimated to a mere 20,000 men by the severe Russian winter and chaos in the ranks. England, Austria, and Prussia then formed an alliance with Russia against Napoleon, who

10   rebuilt his armies and won several minor victories over the Allies, but was soundly defeated in a three-day battle at Leipzig. On March 30, 1814, Paris was captured by the Allies. Napoleon then lost the support of most of his generals and was forced to abdicate on April 6, 1814.

Passage 2

1   Soldiers of my Old Guard: I bid you farewell. For twenty years I have constantly accompanied you on the road to honor and glory. In these latter times, as in the days of our prosperity, you have invariably been models of courage and fidelity. With men such as you our cause could not be lost; but the war would have been interminable; it would have

5   been civil war, and that would have entailed deeper misfortunes on France.
     I have sacrificed all of my interests to those of the country.
     I go, but you, my friends, will continue to serve France. Her happiness was my only thought. It will still be the object of my wishes. Do not regret my fate; if I have consented to survive, it is to serve your glory. I intend to write the history of the great achievements

10   we have performed together. Adieu, my friends. Would I could press you all to my heart.

1. *According to passage 1,*
Ⓐ Napoleon's big mistake was taking his soldiers into Russia.
Ⓑ the French could not be defeated, no matter what Napoleon did.
Ⓒ the Russians were stronger fighters and better armed than the French.
Ⓓ Napoleon's soldiers and generals remained loyal to him until the end.
Ⓔ the effects of this war are still being felt today, nearly 200 years later.

2. *As stated in passage 1, Napoleon retreated because*
Ⓐ he ran out of ammunition.
Ⓑ there was no food for his soldiers.
Ⓒ the weather was too cold.
Ⓓ his soldiers died from battle wounds.
Ⓔ the Russians drove his army out.

3. *How many men did Napoleon lose during the winter?*
Ⓐ 500,000
Ⓑ 20,000
Ⓒ 480,000
Ⓓ 520,000
Ⓔ all of them

4. *As used in passage 1, someone who abdicates*
Ⓐ gives up his or her life.
Ⓑ is kicked out of the military.
Ⓒ joins his or her former enemies.
Ⓓ flees the country in disgrace.
Ⓔ resigns from a position of leadership.

5. *Passage 1 was most likely written by*
Ⓐ Napoleon's speech writer.
Ⓑ one of Napoleon's soldiers.
Ⓒ a Russian general.
Ⓓ Napoleon himself.
Ⓔ an historian.

6. *As used in passage 2, someone who shows fidelity is*
Ⓐ untrustworthy.
Ⓑ happy.
Ⓒ loyal.
Ⓓ angry.
Ⓔ fierce.

7. *Passage 2 was written by*
Ⓐ Napoleon.
Ⓑ a Russian.
Ⓒ a member of the Old Guard.
Ⓓ a modern soldier.
Ⓔ a teacher.

7. *The speaker in passage 2 says all the following but*
Ⓐ I am devoted to my homeland, France.
Ⓑ feel sorry for me because I did not get a fair deal.
Ⓒ thank you for your service and goodbye.
Ⓓ I am proud of the way you fought.
Ⓔ I will write a book about our success.

9. *Unlike passage 1, passage 2*
Ⓐ is unsupported by facts and evidence.
Ⓑ shows a sour and angry writer.
Ⓒ has a malicious and spiteful tone.
Ⓓ has nothing to do with Napoleon.
Ⓔ is written from the first-person point of view.

10. *The authors of these two passages would most likely agree that*
Ⓐ Napoleon did not build an empire for France.
Ⓑ this was the most important war in world history.
Ⓒ the French army never entered Russia.
Ⓓ Napoleon used old-fashioned battle methods.
Ⓔ Napoleon was an important figure in world history.

DIRECTIONS: In this section, solve each problem. You can use any space on the test as scratch paper. Then choose the best answer. Fill in the circle of your answer.

11. *I walked in a straight line 12 blocks from my home, then made a 90° right turn and walked straight for another 5 blocks. If I wanted to walk straight home from here, how far would I have to go?*
Ⓐ 7 blocks
Ⓑ 12 blocks
Ⓒ 13 blocks
Ⓓ 14.5 blocks
Ⓔ 17 blocks

12. **David and Amy baked three pies. If they ate $\dfrac{3}{4}$ of a pie themselves, and served another $1\dfrac{1}{6}$ of a pie to their friends, how many pies are left?**

Ⓐ $\dfrac{1}{12}$ Ⓑ $1\dfrac{1}{12}$ Ⓒ $\dfrac{3}{6}$ Ⓓ $2\dfrac{1}{4}$ Ⓔ 1

13. **Luke's car is fairly fuel-efficient; he gets 32 miles to the gallon. He wants to travel the 230 miles from New York to Baltimore. About how many gallons of gas does he need?**
Ⓐ 6
Ⓑ 8
Ⓒ 10
Ⓓ 15
Ⓔ 23

14. **Which of these fractions is the smallest?**

Ⓐ $\dfrac{3}{7}$ Ⓑ $\dfrac{8}{5}$ Ⓒ $\dfrac{13}{20}$ Ⓓ $\dfrac{14}{5}$ Ⓔ $\dfrac{11}{6}$

15. **Which of the following is a geometric sequence?**
Ⓐ 2, 5, 8, 11...
Ⓑ 1, 1, 2, 3...
Ⓒ 3, 6, 9, 12...
Ⓓ 2, 4, 8, 16...
Ⓔ 4, 16, 24, 36...

DIRECTIONS: Each sentence below is missing one or two words. Under each sentence are possible answers. Choose the answer that best completes each sentence. Fill in the circle of your answer.

16. *Someone who loves liberty has a(n) _____ toward oppression.*
   Ⓐ compassion
   Ⓑ understanding
   Ⓒ sympathy
   Ⓓ empathy
   Ⓔ antipathy

17. *The _____ of secure, well-paying careers today discourages most job-seekers.*
   Ⓐ glut
   Ⓑ scarcity
   Ⓒ profusion
   Ⓓ excess
   Ⓔ wealth

18. *Through his _____, the accountant managed to cheat his clients out of their life savings.*
   Ⓐ ineffiency
   Ⓑ efficiency
   Ⓒ scheming
   Ⓓ competence
   Ⓔ dealings

19. *Although the concert was good, it was overly _____ and the three opening acts were _____.*
   Ⓐ lengthy…thrilling
   Ⓑ brief….exhilarating
   Ⓒ long…excessive
   Ⓓ uplifting…unneeded
   Ⓔ ridiculous…unnecessary

20. *The picnickers waited for the storm to pass, but it _____ refused to end.*
   Ⓐ steadily
   Ⓑ sternly
   Ⓒ weakly
   Ⓓ foolishly
   Ⓔ happily

Answers

Test 1

1. E	6. B	11. D	16. C
2. A	7. C	12. D	17. B
3. B	8. E	13. E	18. A
4. D	9. E	14. D	19. A
5. C	10. A	15. C	20. E

Test 2

1. B	6. B	11. D	16. A
2. C	7. D	12. D	17. C
3. D	8. A	13. A	18. B
4. A	9. B	14. C	19. B
5. E	10. D	15. B	20. E

Test 3

1. A	6. C	11. C	16. E
2. B	7. A	12. B	17. B
3. C	8. B	13. B	18. C
4. D	9. E	14. A	19. C
5. E	10. E	15. D	20. A

Index